KNOTS

AN ILLUSTRATED PRACTICAL GUIDE TO THE ESSENTIAL KNOT TYPES AND THEIR USES

ANDREW ADAMIDES

PLAIN SIGHT PUBLISHING
AN IMPRINT OF CEDAR FORT, INC.
SPRINGVILLE, UT

ISBN 13: 978-1-4621-1400-9

Originally published in 2007 in the United Kingdom by Arcturus Publishing

Published by Plain Sight Publishing, an imprint of Cedar Fort, Inc
2373 W. 700 S., Springville, UT 84663
Distributed by Cedar Fort, Inc., www.cedarfort.com

LIBRARY OF CONGRESS CATALOGING-IN-PUBLICATION DATA

Adamides, Andrew, author.
Knots : an illustrated practical guide to the essential knot types and their uses / Andrew Adamides.
    pages cm
Includes bibliographical references and index.
ISBN 978-1-4621-1400-9 (alk. paper)
1. Knots and splices. I. Title.

GV200.19.K56A43 2014
623.88'82--dc23

2013040472

Cover and interior design by Angela D. Baxter
Cover design © 2014 by Lyle Mortimer
Edited by Whitney Lindsley

Printed in the United States of America

10 9 8 7 6 5 4 3 2 1

Printed on acid-free paper

CONTENTS

INTRODUCTION

This book has been divided into seven main sections, each focusing on one of the different categories of knot. These seven sections are as follows: the first concerns bends; the second, binding knots; the third, hitches; the fourth, loops; the fifth, slip knots; the sixth, splices; and the seventh, stopper knots.

The eighth section is dedicated to trick and fancy knots—the knots featured can of course fall into one of the previous seven sections, but they have been highlighted in this chapter because they have unique characteristics that make them stand out from the crowd. These characteristics vary; some can simply be tied in an unusually fast way, some untie in a distinctive manner. Others are simply very decorative or have uncommon applications.

Each knot type is used for different applications, and each is defined in the individual section introductions. The history, development, uses, strengths, and weaknesses of each individual knot are featured. Each knot also has illustrated step-by-step instructions for tying it. Each individual entry's difficulty level is illustrated through a star rating system, where knots rated with just one star are the easiest, and those with four stars are the hardest.

The book will give the reader a basic overview of each knot, an understanding of its uses and development, and an easy-to-use guide to tying it. It is worth bearing in mind this book can either be dipped Into "one knot at a time" or simply read straight through.

On reading the knot descriptions and instructions, the novice knot-tyer will no doubt notice quickly that there are certain words and terms related to knotting that they may not have previously come across. The glossary section provides definitions for all the knotting terms used within the book. We also provide similar definitions for some basic tools used in knotting and rope work, and an overview of the different types of rope and line.

IMPORTANT NOTICE

While every effort has been taken to ensure the accuracy of the knot illustrations and descriptions featured in this book, it is advised that if you plan to use the knots while in a potentially hazardous or dangerous situation, you should check with a qualified practitioner of knot tying before using the particular knot.

THE HISTORY
OF KNOTS AND ROPE

Ever since man began to use the objects, plants, and creatures around him to make his life easier, he has been tying knots. Indeed, it is widely thought that the first knots were tied in Neolithic times when Neolithic man first tied a stone to a stick, creating a tool or weapon.

Neolithic man's immediate successors proceeded to employ knots to hold together the components used to make shelters and for creating bridges to cross territory that nature had previously made hard or impossible to traverse. And from then on, man became ever more aware of how beneficial knots could be.

Across the planet, new uses were constantly found for knots and rope as various civilizations incorporated them into their daily life. Indeed, rope was considered so important by the Ancient Egyptians that braided and coiled rope was among the objects left in their pharaohs' tombs for use in the afterlife. Archaeologists found such lines in the tomb of Tutankhamen.

The Greeks and Romans put knots to medical use. The earliest written descriptions of knots that still exist date from the fourth century, when doctors of the age wrote of how they used a number of knots to make no fewer than 16 different varieties of slings for broken or wounded limbs. One particular knot described, now known as the Square or Reef Knot and included in this book, was also employed by weapon-makers of the time, as many swords, daggers and similar items excavated by archaeologists used the knot to hold their handles together. Many of these can now be seen in museums worldwide.

Beyond being used to manufacture items, hold things in place, and join objects together, knots have been put to a wide variety of other uses throughout history. In Inca civilizations in Peru, people used string with different knots tied in it instead of writing characters down on paper. Other primitive cultures have linked certain knots with religion, magic, and even curses—with some knots tied to bring ill-fortune and others tied to ward it off.

Knots have also been used for decorative purposes throughout history, be they tied, painted, or molded. The Romans used their form to decorate urns, and they have also appeared molded into the decorative work of buildings throughout history. Lace-making, macramé, and similar crafts have also employed knotting in the creation of fabrics all over the world. And, amazingly, humans are not the only creatures to use knotting for practical purposes—studies have shown that gorillas tie knots in order to hold together branches and vines used to make their nests. Among the knots tied by these highly intelligent creatures are Granny and Reef Knots. Similarly, some birds have been observed tying knots in stalks when building their nests.

With the discovery of knotting came the dawn of rope-making, as archaeological evidence has shown that plant fibers were used by the first knot-tyers, as was catgut, made from the gut of animals slaughtered by these early tribes. Other substances known to have been used in early rope-making include flax, leather, animal hair, and papyrus hemp, which was first used in China around 2800 BC.

As natural fibers obviously decompose over time, very few actual artifacts remain from these early eras, although some very rare pieces are held in museums. The earliest known example of actual manufactured rope is thought to date from around 17,000 BC, when hand-twisted rope was made from plant fibers. Needless to say, this would have been extremely time-consuming. Some ancient Egyptian writings have suggested attempts at creating very simple rope-making machines by finding ways to tie down the strands in order to make twisting them together easier. These inscriptions have been interpreted as depicting the fibers being tied to an already-made rope, or to an object like a dowel or beam. Almost identical methods for rope-making were found in American Indian civilizations dating back to AD 1000. This would be some 5,000 years after the Egyptian inscriptions were made.

As for the substances used in rope-making, the Egyptians mostly employed water-reed fibers. The finished product was of great importance to their society because not only was it thought to be of use in the afterlife, but it was also needed to move the giant, heavy stones used to make the pyramids and other structures.

As rope-making spread across the world, new methods were sought to make its manufacture ever easier. Even the great Leonardo da Vinci designed a rope-making machine, although it never got off the drawing board.

On a more practical level, the Middle Ages saw the introduction of ropewalks; buildings constructed specifically for the purpose of making rope. These buildings were extremely long, and allowed long strands to be laid out flat and then twisted together to make the rope. These ropes could be in excess of 300 yards in length, which meant that there was less need for them to be spliced together for use in the rigging of the sailing ships of the era. Ropewalks could be found across Europe throughout the thirteenth to eighteenth centuries, by which time several functioning rope-making machines had been invented.

As anyone with even a passing knowledge of knotwork and rope-making will know, it is this period that saw the evolution of many of the knots still in use today. Indeed, after the Greek descriptions of the fourth century, the next written descriptions of knots date from the eighteenth century. This period saw more use of sailing ships than ever before, which required huge amounts of rigging in their sails, with miles of rope and numerous knots employed to hold it all together.

At this time, ship voyages took far longer than in later years and the sailors of the day had plenty of free time to while away at sea. Most were unable to either read or write, thus further cutting down even the number of leisure-time activities available to them. However, there was always a lot of rope and line onboard. Using this time to tie and develop new knots became a favorite pastime among sailors, who also named the knots, resulting in some of the more unusually named knots featured in this book.

CHOOSING A KNOT

While each of the different categories of knots included here is applicable in different situations (explained in their individual sections), there are some general criteria to bear in mind when deciding on what knot should be used. First, attention should be paid to the particular knot's strength. Second, working conditions should be considered—will the knot need to be tied quickly and easily or in a confined space? Bear in mind that individual knots work better in some situations than others—particular times to use/not use any one knot are detailed in the individual entries. Last, the size of the finished knot should also be assessed; if it needs to slide through an eye, hole, or similar, obviously a knot that is too large or bulky cannot be used.

ROPE—NATURAL AND ARTIFICIAL

Rope comes in two basic types—natural and artificial. Modern rope can be bought in a huge variety of thicknesses and materials, with its size measured either through its circumference or its diameter. Different thicknesses are referred to by different names—twine, cable, and so on as detailed in the glossary.

Natural rope is made from plant fibers, and for centuries it was the only type of rope available. Plants used in rope-making included manila, sisal, hemp, flax, cotton, and coir, with each different plant type imparting different characteristics to the rope produced from it.

These natural fibers resulted in rope's traditional "hairy" look and rough feel. In some instances, natural rope has the edge over later lines produced from man-made fibers; its roughness means it is easier to grip and less likely to slip. Unfortunately, though, for most practical purposes, the advantages of natural rope are far outweighed by the disadvantages.

Natural-fiber ropes are more prone to damage caused by seawater than their man-made equivalents, since exposure to salt water can cause them to rot. They are also more easily affected by exposure to extended periods of sunlight and to solvents like oil. In addition, they can swell up when wet, which makes them both heavy and cumbersome to move and can also result in a knot becoming very hard to untie.

Ropes made from plant fibers also require more care as they must be cleaned and stored more carefully than synthetic ropes, since they will deteriorate if not clean and dry. In modern times, rope made from natural fibers has been all but supplanted by synthetic rope for practical use. However, it is still sometimes employed for decorative purposes where practicality is not an issue.

Artificial fibers have several advantages over those derived from plants. While individual plant fibers are only as long as the plant they are taken from, man-made fibers can be made in any length and so can run for the whole length of a line. They can also be created to a constant thickness and can be made to adhere to each other without the need for the twisting that natural fibers have. As such, they are stronger than natural-fiber lines.

In addition, man-made fibers do not rot when exposed to seawater or salt, they do not swell when wet, and they have higher resistance to all the conditions that cause wear to natural-fiber ropes. They can also be produced in any color, allowing for the color-coding of various different lines on board ships or boats, for example. They are also better at withstanding shock loading in instances where sudden intermittent force might be placed on a line. Their disadvantages are that they are far smoother than natural-fiber rope, making it easier for knots to slip, and while natural fiber rope can burn when exposed to heat, man-made rope will melt, causing knots to fuse permanently.

Nowadays, man-made rope is manufactured from three particular substances: nylon, polyester, and polypropylene. As with natural fibers from different plants, each of these substances gives rope different characteristics. Nylon ropes have great strength and elasticity. Polyester ropes are marginally less strong, but they do not have as much stretch in them. Polypropylene ropes, meanwhile, are weaker than those made from either nylon or polyester, and cheaper.

It is also worth noting that only polypropylene ropes will float. As such, polypropylene ropes are particularly useful at sea, while nylon or polyester ropes are best used in instances when shock loading is likely—towing a vehicle or mooring a boat, for instance.

ROPE STRUCTURE

Ropes made from natural fibers were created through a process known as "laying up." Essentially, this involves twisting together components made from the constituent plant fibers. The raw fibers would be twisted together to form yarn, the smallest processed component of the rope. The yarn would then be twisted into strands, and these in turn would be twisted together to form rope.

Ropes made from natural fibers are usually three-stranded (i.e., made of three strands twisted together) and are said to be right-laid. This means that if you take such a rope and hold it vertically, you will note that the strands point upward and to your right. This is sometimes referred to as being "Z-Laid," because if you draw two imaginary horizontal lines across the rope, a Z-shape will be formed by these lines and diagonals.

To make a right-laid rope, the plant fibers are initially twisted together to make similar right-handed yarn. This yarn is then twisted together in the opposing direction, making left-laid strands,

and these strands are then twisted together in the opposite direction again, making right-laid rope. Uncoiling one strand of the rope will reveal the left-laid yarn. It is this alternate layering of left and right laying that gives the rope much of its strength.

Rope can also be left-laid, and this is also referred to as being "S-Laid." This method is used to create multi-plait rope. Multi-plait rope has either four or six pairs of strands. Where four are used, two will be right-laid, and the other two left-laid (where six are used, three will be right-laid, and three left-laid) before these are then plaited together to create the rope.

Finally, there is also braided rope, which can be made in a number of different ways using either fibers or filaments. Braided rope features a core at its center, which is either single, plaited, or twisted. A cover goes over this, usually formed from either an eight-plait weave or a 16-plait weave. A final covering layer, usually made in the same way, is then often added over the top of this, using the same construction method.

TOOLS

There are a number of tools that are designed to be used when knotting or undertaking rope work. The specialist tools fids and marlinespikes are mentioned within the text of this book and are defined in our glossary section. However, some other common tools used include the following:

Mallet—mallets are made from either wood or rubber. A medium-sized mallet will be best for most rope work. Mallets are used for shaping rope or for "bedding-down" splices.

Knife—used, obviously enough, for cutting a rope or line. A high-quality knife with a sharp blade is one of the most important parts of any rope worker's kit, but, as with all sharp objects, it should be handled with the utmost care.

Needles—needles used for rope work are large and thick. They can also be used to repair sails, and specialist three-sided needles can be purchased for this, although the casual rope worker can generally make do with a large household needle.

Pliers—these can be used to manipulate rope in instances where it is stiff or where it needs to be bent into a particularly acute shape or where fingers are not strong enough.

Scissors—these can be used as an alternative to a knife for cutting a rope or line. Again, they should be sharp and strong, particularly if they are going to be required to cut through thick line. And, as with knives, care should always be taken when using scissors as they can be highly dangerous when sharp.

ROPE CHOICE AND CARE

Rope suitable for a particular application must always be selected with care. When using newly-purchased rope, make a note of the maker's name, the date on which the rope was produced, its average breaking load and safe working load, its weight, and the material used to make it.

Often this information can be found written on a tape embedded in the rope itself, or on the packaging. If using rope that has already been used, always take into consideration its age, condition and any wear and tear that is apparent. Before using any rope, old or new, you should check it thoroughly for any obvious defects, especially when personal safety may depend on the rope.

To ensure that rope lasts as long as possible, it is suggested that you should avoid having it run tightly over sharp edges or very rough surfaces for extended periods of time. Also, you should avoid stepping on it and forcing it into sharply kinked shapes. Ropes should be stored in coils, and should be dry when put away. They should also be regularly examined for dirt or corrosive substances, which, if found, should be rinsed off. This also applies to salt water, which can be very damaging, especially to natural-fiber ropes.

GLOSSARY

COUNTERCLOCKWISE LOOP

A loop made by leading the working end in the direction against that taken by a clock's hands. Can be either underhand or overhand. See also **Loop**, **Clockwise Loop**, **Overhand Loop**, and **Underhand Loop**.

BIGHT

A section of rope, between the working and standing ends, bent to create a curve or "bump" in the line.

BRAIDING

Interweaving several strands of rope to create a pattern. Sometimes referred to as "plaiting."

BREAKING STRAIN/ STRENGTH

The average load under which a new, never-before-used rope will break, as calculated by the rope's manufacturer.

CABLE

A name generally used for any large rope, although the strict definition deems a cable to be a rope made up of three hawsers laid up together.

CAPSIZE

What happens to a knot when it becomes misshapen, usually from having too much weight placed upon it or not being adequately tightened.

CLOCKWISE LOOP

A loop made by leading the working end in the direction following that of a clock's hands. Can be either underhand or overhand. See also **Loop**, **Counterclockwise Loop**, **Overhand Loop**, and **Underhand Loop**.

CORD

A line made up of several strands of yarn plaited together. In general, this name is applied to lines of diameter under 1 cm (10 mm) only.

DRAW-LOOP

A loop that can be altered in size by pulling on the working end of a line.

EFFICIENCY

Official measure of a knot's strength. This is expressed as a percentage of the breaking strength of the rope.

EYE

A small loop formed in the end of a rope. Also sometimes used as a name for a ring or hole through which line can be threaded.

FIBER

The basic component of a natural-fiber rope.

FID

A small, pointed pin made of wood, used to assist with the loosening of rope strands.

FRAYING

Denotes wear in a rope wherein the rope's separate strands have begun to unravel.

HAWSERS

Large, three-stranded ropes of diameter larger than 1 cm (10mm). Generally used for towing or mooring.

LANYARD

A short length of line used to tie down objects. Often decorated with knots.

LEAD

The direction the working end of a line takes as it goes through a knot, or the action of taking it through the knot.

LINE

A generic name for a rope, cable, or similar. In strictly definitive terms, a line is a rope that has been used for a particular purpose—a clothesline, for example.

LOAD

To place weight on a knot or line. Also the weight under which a knot or line has been placed.

LOCKING TUCK

The final, vital stage of making a particular knot in an instance when, if this step were omitted, the knot would come undone or capsize.

LOOP

A circle made in a rope by passing the working end either under or over the standing part. See also

Counterclockwise Loop, Clockwise Loop, Overhand Loop, and Underhand Loop.

MAKE FAST
To tie a line to an object.

MARLINESPIKE/ MARLINGSPIKE
A metal instrument with a pointed end used to separate rope strands.

OVERHAND LOOP
A loop created in a line by placing the working end over the standing part. Can be either clockwise or counterclockwise. See also counter clockwise Loop, Clockwise Loop, Loop and Underhand Loop.

PLAITING
See Braiding.

REEVING
Passing a rope through an opening such as a hole.

ROUND TURN
A turn in which the working end of a line is passed all the way around a rail, bar or similar object, bringing it back alongside its standing part as it comes out of the turn. See also Turn.

SAFE WORKING LOAD
The average weight that a rope can take without breaking, taking into account the rope's age, its prior usage, and the knots involved. This may be as low as 6% of the manufacturer's previously stated breaking strength. See also Breaking Strength.

SLING
An unbroken circle of rope or similar material.

STANDING END/STANDING PART
The section or end of a line not actively being used in creating a knot. See also Working End.

STRAND
A component of rope, made from twisting yarn together.

TUCK
The act of passing the working end of a line either through a loop or under the standing part to hold it in place.

TURN
One pass of a line around a rail, bar or similar object.

UNDERHAND LOOP

A loop created in a line by placing the working end under the standing part. See also **Counterclockwise Loop, Clockwise Loop, Loop,** and **Overhand Loop.**

WHIPPING

The process of wrapping string or similarly narrow line around the end of a rope to prevent it from fraying.

WORKING END

The end of a line actively being used to create a knot. See also **Standing End/Standing Part.**

YARN

A line created by twisting together fibers. Yarn is then further plaited to create line with a larger diameter.

CHAPTER ONE
BENDS

CHAPTER ONE

BENDS

Definition

A bend is a knot that attaches two lines to each other, end-to-end.

General Purpose and Uses

Bends are, by definition, joining knots. As such, they are used whenever it is necessary to lengthen a piece of rope, cord, string or other similar material by attaching another length to its end. Bends are also used in order to fasten two or more lines to each other in a large loop in order to create a sling or similar lifting device.

Many bends have maritime origins, having been developed for use in the rigging of various types of sails, and many of them date back several centuries—at least one is recorded as being in use as far back as the sixth century. But new variations on the classic bend knot are constantly being developed. While still used in sailing, bends today have countless applications in a wide range of activities from climbing and caving to net-making.

Most bends are designed to join lines of similar diameter and material. Certain more specific types, however, can be used in situations where lines of differing diameter require joining. As with all types of knots, there are various types of bends, each with its own best use—some are better suited to consistent load-bearing, for example, while others are better in situations where the line, once tied, will be subject to strain that varies in angle and consistency, such as that exerted by a boat tied to a dock.

Characteristics of a Bend

Bends are generally considered to be temporary knots in that they can usually be untied and the material used to tie them reused. That said, some are more easily untied than others, so the use of harder-to-release bends should be limited to situations in which the knot is intended as a permanent fixture (although a shroud knot or splice is generally better suited to permanent joins). As a rule of thumb, bends utilizing a thick tie line are easier to untie; those with a finer tie line tend to be more permanent.

While bends joining lengths of similar material are usually strong and stable knots, those that unite lines that differ in size, texture, or flexibility can be significantly weaker—although certain types of bends are better suited to this latter use than others. In many cases, bends tying different types of material together display similar characteristics to hitches.

Although they may appear to be a viable alternative, binding knots should never be used in place of bends, as they are far more likely to slip. It should also be noted that, while some bends are stronger than others, some will cause a certain amount of wear to the lines involved—a fact that should be taken into account when deciding which type of bend to employ.

SHEET BEND

DIFFICULTY: 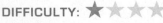 ★★★★

HISTORY

The Sheet Bend makes its first recorded appearance in seamanship books of the late eighteenth century, the writers of which naming it after the fact that its primary use was in securing the trimming ropes, or sheets, that were attached to ships' sails. Another popular use of the Sheet Bend was attaching flags to masts, at which times it was commonly referred to as the Flag Bend.

The Sheet Bend is closely related to the Beckett Hitch, which is essentially the same knot but used to tie a line to an eye or similar circular locator, rather than simply joining two lines. As such, it is also sometimes referred to as the Beckett Bend. A further variation on the standard Sheet Bend was documented in 1990, when a member of the International Guild of Knot Tyers recorded the Three-Way Sheet Bend, as seen in the Greek port of Gaios. This version differs from the standard Sheet Bend in that it joins three lengths of line rather than two.

BEST USES

Quick to make and easy to untie, the Sheet Bend works well in joining lines of varying thickness or material. It is stable when placed under moderate stress, but it is not known for its strength. The knot works best with lines that are not too stiff, and, if necessity calls for it to be used in conjunction with stiff lines or those that are wet or slippery, it should be made into a Double Sheet Bend for extra strength. This knot is widely employed in the construction of nets.

HOW TO MAKE A SHEET BEND

The Sheet Bend should always be started with the thicker of the two lines being joined. It is tied as follows:

STEP 1

Taking the thicker line (Line A), form a bight with the working end, bringing it up and alongside its standing part. Hold the working end of Line A in place to form an eye in the line before bringing the working end of the thinner line (Line B) into range and then threading it through the eye of Line A.

STEP 2

Pass the working end of Line B back under both the working end of Line A and Line A's standing part.

STEP 3

Bring the working end of Line B back across the top of the eye, passing over both sides of the loop and under itself in the process. Finally, pull on both standing parts to tighten.

THE CARRICK BEND

DIFFICULTY RATING: ★ ★ ★ ★

HISTORY

With numerous variations on its basic form, a long history, and some lively debate regarding the origins of its name, the Carrick Bend is one of the most remarkable bend knots in existence.

The Carrick Bend is first found recorded in a French book of seafaring terminology published in 1883, although its first appearance in English dates from 1922, when it appeared in the book *Seamanship for the Merchant Service*.

While the knot's inventor remains unknown, there are a number of conflicting theories on where its name comes from. The most popular is that the knot was named after a type of ship, the carrack, dating from medieval times and widely used across western Europe. Others point to the fact that the decorative Elizabethan plasterwork of Ormonde Castle in Ireland's Carrick-on-Suir features a number of Carrick Bends molded into the relief; the plasterwork dates from between 1558 and 1603, so this may be where the knot originally picked up its enigmatic moniker. Finally, a third theory links the knot with Carrick Roads, a bay near Falmouth in Cornwall. Whatever the truth behind the debate, it's interesting to note that the Wake Knot, a variation on the Carrick Bend, was the heraldic badge of Hereward the Wake, a Saxon leader who revolted against William the Conqueror in 1071.

VARIATIONS

The Carrick Bend is often tied incorrectly, which has, in the past, led to numerous less reliable knots being erroneously labelled as Carrick Bends. That said, a "true" or "full" Carrick Bend can be easily identified through the behavior of the lines at each of its eight crossing points, which alternate between passing over and under.

There are two basic variations on the true Carrick Bend: the Carrick Bend with Ends Opposed and the Carrick Bend with Ends Adjacent. In the case of the former, the ends of the two pieces of rope or cord emerge on opposite sides of the knot; in the latter, they come out on the same side. The Carrick Bend with Ends Opposed is widely accepted as the stronger of the two variations, while the other is more decorative, popular with designers and artists, who—like Hereward the Wake and the designers of Ormonde Castle—have throughout history seized on its artful symmetry for inspiration. The knot has been incorporated into fields as diverse as architecture, stationery design, braiding, and macramé, and has several variant names within creative circles: macramé makers refer to it as the Josephine Knot, braiders as a Check Knot, and fans of Chinese knotting know it as the Double Coin Knot.

BEST USES

While its artistic applications are many, the Carrick Bend is most practically useful in joining together large ropes, cables, or similar lines, and can also be used in uniting lines with slightly varying thicknesses. Although it has a reputation for strength, even the sturdier Carrick Bend with Ends Opposed can have an efficiency rating of as low as 65%, and if the ends of the knot are not seized, then the bend will "collapse"—leaving it workable but extremely difficult to untie. This unfortunate failing can also occur when the knot is wet or subjected to heavy stress.

BENDS

HOW TO MAKE A CARRICK BEND

Both variations of the Carrick Bend are fairly easy to accomplish. For the Carrick Bend with Ends Opposed, tie as follows:

STEP 1

Take the line on your right (Line A) and form a counterclockwise over-hand loop with the working end.

STEP 2

Place the working end of the line on your left (Line B) diagonally over the loop and sloping downward from left to right. At a point to the right of the loop, pass it under the standing part of Line A and over the working end.

STEP 3

Bring the working end of Line B back diagonally through the loop (sloping downward from right to left), in the process going under both sides and over itself. Pull both standing parts to tighten.

The Carrick Bend with Ends Adjacent, meanwhile, is tied by more or less reversing the opposite instructions:

STEP 1

Taking the line on your right (Line A), form a clockwise overhand loop with the working end.

STEP 2

Place the working end of the line on your left (Line B) diagonally underneath the loop and sloping downward from left to right. At a point to the right of the loop, pass the working end of Line B over the working end of Line A and under Line A's standing part.

STEP 3

Bring the working end of Line B back diagonally through the loop (sloping downward from right to left) before passing it over both sides of the loop and under itself. This knot will look most decorative when left flat and open rather than pulled tight.

FISHERMAN'S KNOT

DIFFICULTY: ★ ☆ ☆ ☆

HISTORY

The Fisherman's Knot might well win the prize for the knot with the most variant names, having no less than eight different aliases in total. It may also be one of the oldest knots in existence, with some sources claiming that it was first utilized in ancient Greece, although most people now agree that it is a more recent creation than that.

The knot's first confirmed usage came in the early nineteenth century, when it was employed, perhaps not surprisingly, by fishermen, who knew it as the Angler's Knot, although it has since been referred to variously as the English Knot, the Englishman's Knot, the True Lover's Knot, the Water Knot, the Waterman's Knot, and even the Halibut Knot.

BEST USES

The Fisherman's Knot is most commonly used to tie together fine line or thin pieces of rope of similar or equal diameters—a fact that makes it ideal for joining lengths of fishing line, the purpose for which it was most likely invented and from which its most popular name is derived.

When thicker lines are involved, the Fisherman's Knot becomes easier to untie; the thinner the lines being used, the greater the likelihood that they will need to be cut in order to separate them again. When tied in thin lines and pulled tight, the knot becomes extremely small, and, although the knot is both strong and secure in itself, the act of tying it will considerable weaken the lines involved—a fact that should be considered before making any attempt to reuse them.

HOW TO MAKE A FISHERMAN'S KNOT

It should be noted that the Fisherman's Knot and the Fisherman's Bend are two different knots. Confusingly, the Fisherman's Bend is in fact a hitch and not a bend, while the Fisherman's Knot, described here, is a bend.

The Fisherman's Knot consists of two identical overhand knots wrapped around each other, and is tied as follows:

STEP 1

Place the two lines parallel, one above the other, with the ends facing in opposite directions.

STEP 2

Take the working end of the upper line (Line A) and form a clockwise overhand loop, encompassing the standing part of the lower line (Line B), going first under, then over Line B.

STEP 3

Pass the working end of Line A back over its own standing part before passing it back through the loop, taking it first under and then over itself, so that it faces in the same direction as it did initially.

STEP 4

Take the working end of Line B and repeat the above: form a clockwise overhand loop encompassing the standing part of Line A, going under, then over. Pass it back over its own standing part, then take it under, over back through the loop. Pull both standing parts to tighten.

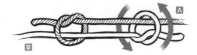

A completed Fisherman's Knot

BENDS

FLEMISH BEND

DIFFICULTY: ★ ★ ☆ ☆

HISTORY

The exact origins of the Flemish Bend are unknown, although it is believed to have originated in mainland Europe, where it was employed for mostly nautical purposes. By the mid-twentieth century, the knot had fallen out of favor both with sailors and knot enthusiasts alike, who deemed it too bulky and cumbersome to tie, and tired of its tendency to jam when used in conjunction with natural fiber ropes.

This latter problem was largely alleviated by the advent of modern synthetic ropes, which led to a resurgence in the popularity of the Flemish Bend, and the knot was subsequently counted by the Surrey, England, branch of the International Guild of Knot Tyers as one of their six most important knots. Due to its shape, the Flemish Bend is also occasionally known as a Figure Eight Bend.

BEST USES

The Flemish Bend is most widely used in climbing, a field in which it excels thanks to its strength, stability and the ease with which team leaders can check that it has been tied properly. In addition, it is also relatively easy to untie, especially when used with thicker lines, and this remains the case even after it has been subjected to consider-able stress. It is unlikely to jam and causes less wear than many bends to the lines used to tie it, allowing them to be resused with a considerable amount of confidence. The Flemish Bend works best with lines of medium thickness and can be used in conjunction with fairly slick material. The only downside is that it can be rather bulky.

HOW TO MAKE A
FLEMISH BEND

This knot is strong in itself, although double overhand stopper knots should be tied on each side if they are to be used to support a person in any potentially dangerous situation.

STEP 1

Take the line on your right (Line A) and form a clockwise overhand loop with the working end. Taking hold of the loop, twist it upward, forming a "figure eight" in the line.

STEP 2

Pass the working end back through the left-most loop of the figure eight formed by the above action (the loop furthest to your left), taking it under, then over, so it exits pointing to your left.

STEP 3

Take the line on your left (Line B) and bring the working end into the left-most loop, parallel to Line A. Follow the lead of Line A, and pass Line B through the knot. Line B should go in an over-under-over-under-over pattern through the figure eight. When the working end of Line B has been threaded all the way alongside the first, tighten by pulling on each working end.

HUNTER'S BEND

DIFFICULTY:

HISTORY

The Hunter's Bend enjoyed a seemingly high-profile launch in 1978, when it appeared on the front page of the *Times* newspaper as a newly discovered knot credited to one Dr. Edward Hunter. He was said to have been using it to repair snapped shoelaces for several years before a friend made him aware of its "originality."

Later research, however, revealed that the same knot had previously appeared in a book entitled *Knots for Mountaineering*, published in the mid-1950s, the author of which—an American named Phil Smith—had in fact created the knot a decade or so earlier, calling it a Rigger's Bend. Regardless, the 1978 "discovery" led to the establishment of the International Guild of Knot Tyers in 1982.

BEST USES

Square in shape and extremely stable, the Hunter's Bend is used in sailing and, to a lesser extent, in climbing. Like the Flemish Bend, it is both easy to untie and very well suited to modern, synthetic ropes. It also works well with rope or line that is stiff or slippery, and with flexible line such as bungee cord. It works best when joining lines of similar or equal diameter that are not too thick.

HOW TO MAKE A HUNTER'S BEND

The Hunter's Bend is closely related to the Zeppelin Bend. It is tied as follows:

STEP 1

Position the two lines to be joined so one (Line A) is above the other (Line B), with the working ends facing in opposite directions. Make a clockwise overhand loop in the working end of Line A.

STEP 2

Take the working end of Line B, and make a counterclockwise underhand loop. Position the loop in Line B so it overlaps the loop in Line A. Position the working end of Line B under the working end of Line A.

STEP 3

Take the working end of Line A and pass it back through both loops, taking it in an under-over pattern. Then, take the working end of Line B and pass that through both loops, taking it in an over-under pattern. Gently remove the slack, then alternately pull each working end and standing part until the knot is fully tightened.

VICE VERSA

DIFFICULTY RATING: ★★☆☆

HISTORY

The Vice Versa is another example of a knot that is widely regarded as being a fairly recent creation, but that which may well have a far longer history behind it.

The knot made what was at the time accepted as its first appearance in a 1986 book, *A New System of Knotting*, and the author of which was credited with its creation. However, ten years later, another book, *The History and Science of Knots*, unearthed a 1928 issue of climber's magazine *The Alpine Journal*, which contained a description of the same knot, then known as the Reaver Knot.

And yet, the Vice Versa may go back even further than that. In the mid 1970s, explorer Tim Severin built a replica of the cowhide boat used by St. Brendan in the sixth century and used this knot to join the boat's leather body panels together. Severin noted in an article that the knot had been chosen because it closely resembled the one in sixth-century manuscripts, and may even have been the one used by St. Brendan himself.

BEST USES

The Vice Versa is best suited to joining lines that have a slick or slippery surface, whether this is natural or due to the surrounding conditions. Thanks to its unique construction, it is also useful when working with elasticized material, making it a natural choice for joining bungee cords or modern synthetic ropes. The knot is both fairly stable and easy to undo. It is also relatively small, and as such is useful in situations where the line needs to pass through an eye or similar circular mooring.

BENDS

BENDS

HOW TO MAKE A
VICE VERSA
The Vice Versa is tied as follows:

STEP 1

Position the two lines to be joined one above the other, with the working ends facing in opposite directions. The line with its working end pointing to your left (Line A) should be below the line with its working end pointing to your right (Line B). Take the working end of Line B and form a clockwise underhand loop, taking it first under, then over Line A's standing part as you do so.

STEP 2

Take the working end of Line A and form a counterclockwise overhand loop, taking it first over, then under Line B's standing part as you do so. Both working ends should now be next to each other and pointing upward.

STEP 3

Cross the working end of Line B over the working end of Line A. Pass the working end of Line A through the loop to your right, going first under then over. Repeat this action with the working end of Line B, passing it through the loop to your left, going first under and then over, and finally pull all ends to tighten.

BENDS

ZEPPELIN BEND

DIFFICULTY RATING: ★ ★ ★ ☆

HISTORY

The Zeppelin Bend takes its name from the dirigible airships, popular in the early part of the twentieth century, the knot being used to tie them to their moorings. It is also sometimes known as the Rosendahl Bend after Lieutenant Commander Charles Rosendahl of the United States Navy, who captained the airship *Los Angeles* and refused to employ any other type of knot on board—whether for tying lines or mooring the ship itself.

BEST USES

The Zeppelin Bend is known for its security and the veritable impossibility of it jamming. As such, it is ideal for use with heavy-duty lines or ropes, and, while there may be little call for tethering airships today, it is nevertheless perfect for use in mooring boats because of its ability to cope with heavy loads and stress, even when the latter is not constant or continuous. The knot can generally be untied fairly easily, although it may require somewhat more effort if it has been placed under stress.

HOW TO MAKE A ZEPPELIN BEND

Rosendahl's original method for tying the Zeppelin Bend was significantly more complex than the modern method, which is described here:

STEP 1

Take the two lines to be joined, placing Line A above Line B so that both working ends point in the same direction. Taking the working end of Line B, form an overhand loop, going over both lines.

STEP 2

As it emerges from the loop, thread the working end of Line B back through the loop, taking it under both itself and Line A, then over.

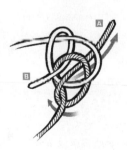

STEP 3

Taking the working end of Line A, form an underhand loop, then pass it back over itself and through the loop formed by Line B, going over Line B then under both Line B and itself as it exits the loop.

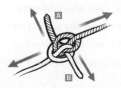

STEP 4

Hold the working ends and the standing parts together, and pull on both to tighten the knot.

CHAPTER TWO
BINDING KNOTS

CHAPTER TWO

BINDING KNOTS

DEFINITION

A Binding Knot is one tied into a line for the purpose of holding an object or objects together or in place.

GENERAL PURPOSE AND USES

Binding knots are useful in any situation where a single item needs to be held in place or a number of items bound together. As such, binding knots are used for everything from securing groups of metal poles to tying up wrapping paper on parcels and even the compression of bandages by doctors. Many such knots date back centuries, although they've been much improved upon over the years, while others are more recent creations.

Binding knots vary greatly in their strengths, and different variations are, as always, suited to different materials and applications. It should be noted, however, that it is always highly unadvisable to use binding knots in place of bends as they are neither designed for, nor suited to the same purposes, especially in potentially dangerous situations.

CHARACTERISTICS OF BINDING KNOTS

Binding knots can be divided into two distinct categories differenti-ated by their basic forms. In the case of the first, sometimes referred to as the Friction Type, the line being used to tie the knot is wound round the object to be held in place several times and then passed under itself. This creates internal friction, which in turn holds the knot together. The second category, known as the Knotted Ends Type, requires the line to be wound around the objects to be tied and the ends then knotted together to secure the object.

Each category is suited to different types of application; the Friction Type is best employed when the items to be bound are of narrow diameter—in clamping a hosepipe to a tap, for example. The Knotted Ends Type works best for objects with wider diam-eters, such as when securing or compressing bandages to arms or legs.

Binding knots vary greatly in strength, from the very secure to the easily untied, and can be used for both semipermanent and tem-porary purposes. Generally speaking, binding knots are best tied with two ends of the same piece of line, although they can also be tied using two separate pieces of similar material. They are not recommended for use with two lines that differ greatly in thickness or texture.

REEF KNOT

DIFFICULTY: ★ ☆ ☆ ☆

HISTORY

While a number of the knots covered in this book date back a long way, it is unlikely that any of them predate the trusted Reef Knot. It's an equally safe bet that few knots are used quite so often: even those unaware of the Reef Knot's existence will regularly use it to tie their shoelaces. It is also among the simplest of knots to tie—arguably the simplest of them all.

The earliest known examples of the Reef Knot crop up as far back as 10,000 years ago, used as it was by Neolithic-era man, as well as by the ancient Egyptians, Greeks, and Romans. One of the earliest surviving examples of a Reef Knot can be found at the Pecos Rio Grande Museum of Early Man in Texas, where two primitive ropes made of lechugilla, a plant fiber, are tied together using this same knot in an artifact dating back several thousand years. Reef Knots can also be seen depicted on ancient Roman pottery, and there is evidence that the Chinese may have employed the knot during the Tang and Song Dynasty, from AD 960 to 1229. Nowadays, it is immortalized on the International Membership Badge for Boy Scouts.

The knot has had several names during the course of its lifetime. Americans currently refer to it as the Square Knot thanks to its shape, while the ancient Romans knew it as the Hercules Knot. Back then, the knot was popular with the Roman scholar Pliny the Elder, who claimed that it actually helped speed up the healing of a wound when used to secure a bandage. It remains in use throughout the medical world (in such cases known as the First Aid Knot), although its more common moniker Reef Knot derives from its maritime use in anchoring sails: it could easily be weakened with one hand, after which the sail's weight would pull it apart naturally, which in turn would fold back or "reef" the sail, hence the name.

BEST USES

Beside its obvious use in fastening the likes of shoelaces and belts, the Reef Knot has many other applications. It is best employed in situations where it is joining together the ends of one line to hold an object in place, and where such fastening is not intended to be permanent. It is also used often in macramé and, as mentioned earlier, for securing bandages and slings. It is also commonly used to tie garbage bags.

Although easy to tie, the Reef Knot is not known for its strength. As such, it can be used as a general purpose binding knot, but it should only be employed when it can be tied in such a way that the completed knot lies snugly against the surface of whatever it is securing. Under no circumstances should the knot be used in place of a bend, as it will give a false impression of strength before quickly unraveling. In addition to this, it should never be used in a situation where reliance on it places life in the balance. This viewpoint has been endorsed by the International Guild of Knot Tyers, with some sources claiming that the failure of Reef Knots when employed in the wrong situations has been responsible for more deaths than all other knots put together.

Lastly, it should be noted that Reef Knots work best when tied using the opposite ends of either the same or similar lines; if there is any difference between the lines in terms of texture, thickness or stiffness, this will weaken the knot considerably.

HOW TO MAKE A
REEF KNOT

The Reef Knot is incredibly fast and simple to tie, although care needs to be taken to avoid tying a less stable Granny Knot by mistake. A Knotted Ends Type Binding Knot, it is tied as follows:

STEP 1

Taking the two ends of your line, place the end on your left (End A) over the end on your right (End B).

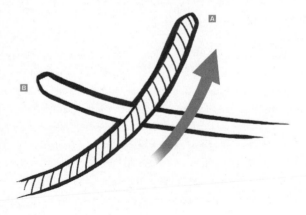

A completed Reef Knot

STEP 2

Take End A under and then over the standing part of End B. Take End B over and then under the standing part of End A.

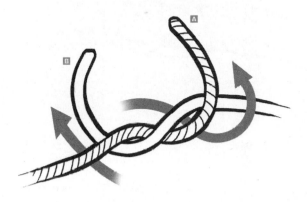

STEP 3

With both ends pointing upward, cross End A over End B. Take End A under and then over the standing part of End B. Bring End B over and then under the standing part of End A and pull to tighten.

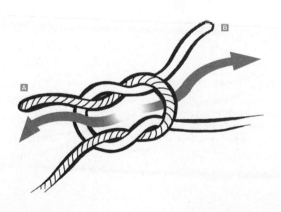

GRANNY KNOT

DIFFICULTY: ★ ☆ ☆ ☆

HISTORY

In short, the Granny Knot is a Reef Knot gone wrong. As such, it is technically a derivative of the Reef Knot and presumably has as extensive a history; for as long as humans have been tying Reef Knots—which is more or less as long as there have been humans to tie them—they have most likely been mistakenly making Granny Knots as well. As a result of its reputation for coming apart, it is also sometimes known as the Slipknot.

BEST USES

The Granny Knot is, all told, pretty useless. The only time when it might actually come into its own is on those rare occasions where a knot is required that can come apart at the merest pull—although its tendency to jam makes it rather unsuitable even then. As such, we include it here more as a warning than an instruction: by understanding how it is formed, one can avoid making it accidentally and recognize when others have made it by mistake. The knot is most commonly found in poorly tied shoelaces, in which cases it almost always results in the loops of the bow coming undone and the knot itself needing to be picked apart with fingernails to much annoyance.

HOW TO MAKE A GRANNY KNOT

In order to understand how to avoid making a Granny Knot in error, read the following instructions and then contrast them with those for the Reef Knot on the previous pages. For the record, the Granny Knot is a Knotted Ends Bind, and is formed thus:

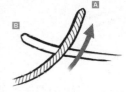

STEP 1

Taking the two ends of your line, place the end on your left (End A) over the end on your right (End B).

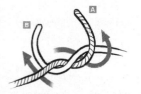

STEP 2

Pass End A under and then over the standing part of End B. Pass End B over and then under the standing part of End A.

STEP 3

With both ends pointing upward, cross End B over End A. Pass End B under and then over the standing part of End A. Pass End A over and then under the standing part of End B and pull to tighten.

MILLER'S KNOT

DIFFICULTY: ★ ★ ★ ★

HISTORY

The Miller's Knot, also known as the Sack Knot, is another binding knot with a lengthy history. It was first used several hundred years ago by millers to seal large bags of flour and continues to be used for this original purpose today, although it can also be found employed in any other industry that requires the tying off of bags and sacks.

BEST USES

The knot's suitability for securing bags and sacks stems from the fact that it is semipermanent, but it can be loosened and tightened with relative ease and with little or no loss of strength. As such, it allows the user access to the contents of the sack and allows him or her to reseal it after more has been added or removed, with no loss of security. In addition to being used for tying off sacks, the knot is commonly used to tie hay bales and by hikers and campers securing their bags to tree branches to keep them off the ground.

HOW TO MAKE A MILLER'S KNOT

The Miller's Knot bears a great resemblance to the Clove Hitch. The following description is for the frequent instance of tying it around the neck of a bag or sack (whenever it is being used to secure any other sort of material, simply substitute this item in place of the sack neck):

STEP 1

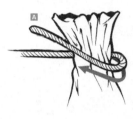

Position your line behind the sack's neck, with the neck closer to one end of the line than the other. Take the shorter end (End A) and make a turn over the neck. Hold End A so that it points upward and in the same direction as the opening of the sack.

STEP 2

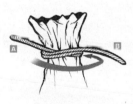

Take the longer end of the line (End B) and make a round turn about the sack neck, passing it over End A as you do so and thus trapping End A in place.

STEP 3

Going first over and then under, pass End B through the eye created by End A and thus trap it in place. Pull tight.

BOA KNOT

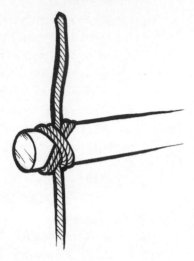

DIFFICULTY: ★★★★

HISTORY

The Boa Knot's history is far shorter than most of the knots described in this book, being just ten years old at the time of this book's first printing. The knot was invented in 1996 by a weaver and writer named Peter Collingwood, who aimed to find a knot suitable for securing objects together when it was intended that those objects would then be cut through. The Boa Knot's basic form is closely related to both the earlier Strangle Knot and Double Constrictor Knot, with its name a play on the latter and a nod to the way in which it winds around objects like a Boa Constrictor.

BEST USES

As previously noted, the Boa Knot was devised with the aim of holding together objects due to be cut through and keeping them together after this action has taken place. As such, the knot works best when used to tie together numerous long, thin objects in a cylindrical bundle—poles, for example, or sticks. The knot is strong, secure, and straightforward to tie.

HOW TO MAKE A BOA KNOT

The Boa Knot is easy and quick to tie. It is a friction knot and is best suited to securing thin objects.

STEP 1

Make an overhand loop in the center of your line. Then, create a second overhand loop to the left of the first.

STEP 2

Place the second loop on top of the first, and position both ends of the line so they point upward. This should form a three-deep coil.

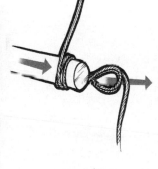

STEP 3

Taking hold of either side of this coil, twist the right-hand side upward, to form a figure eight. Pass the object you wish to secure through this figure eight, bringing it in from the left. Pass it under the end of the loop, over the point where the loops cross, then under the right-side end of the loop.

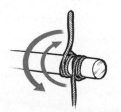

STEP 4

Pass the ends of the line under the diagonals and pull tight to secure.

CONSTRICTOR KNOT

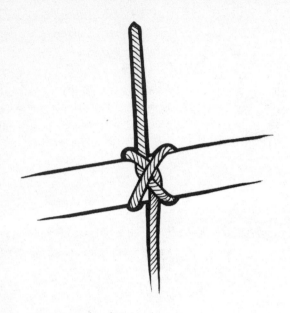

DIFFICULTY: ★★☆☆

HISTORY

In contrast to the Boa Knot, the Constrictor Knot from which it derives has a long history, dating far back into the twentieth century—and possibly much, much further.

The knot appears in Clifford Ashley's seminal knot book, 1944's *Ashley Book of Knots*, in which Ashley himself takes credit for having invented it some 25 years prior to the book's publication. However, research by the International Guild of Knot Tyers has revealed that the Constrictor Knot may well be the same as one referred to in writings by the ancient Greek physician Heraklas, produced almost two thousand years earlier in the first century AD. This cannot be proved for certain, sadly, as there are no pictures or diagrams to support Heraklas's descriptions in the relevant text, which is concerned with the making of slings to support the arm.

The Constrictor Knot's next notable appearance came during the nineteenth century against a more warlike backdrop. An 1890 text describes what appears to be the Constrictor Knot being used as a method for sealing flannel bags filled with gunpowder, thus making them into rudimentary cartridges for use in early cannons. Slightly later, a 1916 volume hailing from Sweden identified the knot as the Timber Knot, and it made a subsequent appearance in the same region in 1931, when the Finnish girl scout leader Marta Ropponen included it in her own illustrated book of knots. Ropponen quoted a Spanish friend of hers, Raphael Gaston, who had reputedly informed her of the knot's common use by animal herders In the Spanish mountains.

Ashley, It seems, did not create the Constrictor Knot after all, but he almost certainly did more than Heraklas, Ropponen, or anyone else to boost its popularity, featuring it in his *Ashley Book of Knots* no less than 13 times.

BEST USES

The Constrictor Knot is extremely versatile—some suggest that it has more diverse uses than any other single knot—and in its various forms has been widely recognized as one of the knots that a novice should learn to tie first. Its versatility derives largely from the fact that it can be tied using almost any line, and so can be used in a wide range of situations and applications. For example, it is ideal when sealing a sack, soft bag, or similar item with a cord, or for attaching line to a nail or other protruding object, but it is equally at home providing temporary whipping for the end of a rope or holding bundles of objects or other lines together.

The knot is extremely secure and easy to tie. It can be used as either a temporary or permanent knot, but should generally not be used with soft or easily damaged materials that need to retain their appearance, as it is notorious for leaving track marks.

HOW TO MAKE A CONSTRICTOR KNOT

The Constrictor Knot is also a friction knot. It can be tied in several variations, the simplest of which is as follows:

STEP 1

Take your length of line, and lay it over the object to be secured. Make a round turn around the object. As the working end comes out of the turn, bring it to one side of the standing part.

STEP 2

Cross the working end over the standing part and take it through another round turn about the object. Bring it out of the turn on the other side of the standing part to your first turn. Pass the working end under the diagonal where the first turn crosses the standing part.

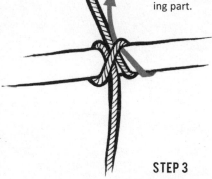

STEP 3

Pass the working end over the initial turn. Then, take hold of the initial turn and pull to loosen slightly. Pass the working end through this, so that, as it exits from under the diagonal, it goes in an over-under-over pattern in relation to the first turn. Pull both ends to tighten.

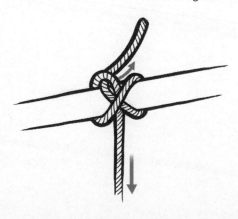

BINDING KNOTS

CHAPTER THREE
HITCHES

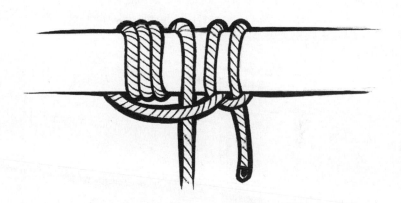

CHAPTER THREE

HITCHES

DEFINITION

Hitches are knots that fasten a line to an immovable object, such as a horizontal rail, vertical post, or ring.

GENERAL PURPOSE AND USES

Hitches are exclusively used for tying lines to immovable objects. As such, their uses include the tethering of animals, the mooring of small boats, and the tying of rigging or sails aboard ships. Strangely enough, lines fastened to objects using hitches are never referred to as being "hitched" but rather "made fast"—even in cases where the line is tied to the center of another line or rope. Many hitches were developed on board ships, and date from a time when more seagoing craft had sails and rigging than do so today.

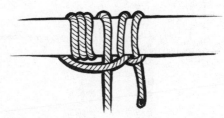

There are many different types of hitches, each of which will work best for different applications. Some, for example, work better under conditions in which the force exerted on the line used to tie them is at right angles to the object to which it is attached; others are better suited to applications in which the pull will be intermittent in force and its angle will vary. Further distinctions can be made between hitches that are best suited for tying to upright bollards, around rings, or for tethering to horizontal beams, while some are notable for being easier to untie than others, especially when wet or in unfavorable conditions.

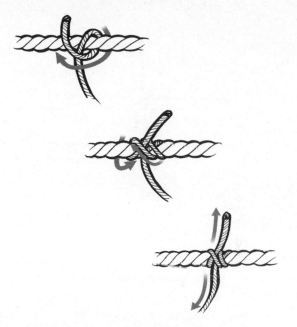

CHARACTERISTICS OF HITCHES

Hitches are designed to hold when force is exerted on the rope used to tie them, and can be tied in almost any material. Their strength obviously varies dramatically, but some of the most basic hitches are very weak. Most are also impermanent; while they will generally not come undone when force is exerted on the line used to tie them, they can usually be untied when the proper steps to do so are taken, although some hitches will be more difficult to unravel than others.

Interestingly, hitches can also be used to attach two lines together, but not in the same way as a bend. A hitch can be used in any instance where one line is being tied to the center of another, at which times they differ structurally from bends in that they involve wrapping the second line around the first, rather than knotting the two together. As such, hitches should never be used in place of a bend, as they will not hold, nor should a bend be attempted in any situation where a hitch is required.

CLOVE HITCH

DIFFICULTY: ★ ★ ★ ★

HISTORY

The Clove Hitch is a simple knot that has been around for a very long time. It is of maritime origin, and was known by various names up until the eighteenth century, including the Waterman's Knot, Lark's Head Crossed, and Builder's Knot. The last of these is still in use by non-nautical types today, although the more prevalent name Clove Hitch appears to have been coined by William Falconer in his 1769 book, *The Universal Dictionary of the Marine*. At that time, the knot was used on square-rigged ships, particularly to manufacture ladders out of rope that were then used by sailors to reach the upper masts.

BEST USES

The Clove Hitch is not strong, and its tendency to slip or jam at inopportune moments means that it should never be used in any important or life-threatening applications. It works better with lines that are thick and rugged rather than thin or slick-surfaced; on thinner, slippery lines it will come loose far more easily. To be fair, the only situations in which the Clove Hitch is of any real use are those in which equal or near-equal loads are applied to either end of the cord in which it is tied—in any other situation, it will almost certainly come loose.

HITCHES

HOW TO MAKE A
CLOVE HITCH

There are two variants of the Clove Hitch: one for tying a line around an upright post; the other for tying it to a horizontal bar, ring, or similar.

For tethering to a post, the knot is tied as follows:

STEP 1

Take your line and make an overhand loop, then form an underhand loop to the right of the initial overhand loop.

STEP 2

Place the underhand loop on top of the overhand loop. Place the two loops over the post and pull both ends of the rope to tighten.

For tethering to a horizontal bar or similar, the knot is tied as follows:

STEP 1

Pass your line around the bar you wish to tie it to, bringing the working end under the bar and crossing it up over the standing part.

STEP 2

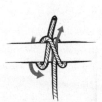

Pass the working end over and around the bar again. Bring it out under the bar, and tuck it under its own standing part. Pull to tighten.

HALF HITCH

DIFFICULTY: ★★★★

HISTORY

The exact history of the Half Hitch has never been recorded, largely because it has been around for centuries and is one of the easiest knots to tie. Nevertheless, its form and application mark it out very much as being a hitch, and it has a lot of use as a strengthening knot when used in combination with other knots.

BEST USES

While easy to tie in almost any line, the Half Hitch is not particularly strong when used on its own, and has a tendency to unravel in all but the best conditions. However, it is extremely useful as a fortifying knot when applied to the working end of another hitch, and can thus either hold the other hitch in place or make its bond stronger, depending on the circumstances. The Clove Hitch is one example of a hitch that can benefit from the addition of a Half Hitch (although it can also be applied to any type of knot where there is leftover length in the working end). The Half Hitch is also a very attractive knot, and is widely used in the creation of French Whipping and in other creative pursuits. The knot can be tied as either a single knot or as Two Half Hitches, with the latter being significantly stronger.

HOW TO MAKE A
HALF HITCH

The Half Hitch is exceedingly simple to tie—so much so, in fact, that many people will have used it countless times in the past without even knowing its name. When using it to anchor a line directly to a bar or similar object, it is tied as follows (to add it to another knot, simply omit looping the line around the bar):

STEP 1

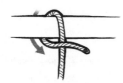

Pass your line over the bar. Bring the working end over the standing part.

STEP 2

Tuck the working end through the turn formed by the line and pull tight.

STEP 3

To form Two Half Hitches, tie as above, then pass the working end around the standing part again, taking it first over, then under the standing part, and finally passing it back over itself. Pull to tighten.

FISHERMAN'S BEND

DIFFICULTY: ★ ☆ ☆ ☆

HISTORY

The Fisherman's Bend, also known as the Anchor Bend, is rather misleadingly named. It is most definitely not a bend, and is highly unsuitable for use as one; it is, rather, a hitch. Its name was initially coined by sailors who used it to tie lines to mooring rings, known in the vernacular of the time as "bending" the line to the ring. It seems to have stuck, and has been confusing people ever since thanks to its appearances in the books *Elements and Practice of Seamanship* (1794) and *The Handbook of Sailing* (1904).

BEST USES

As the sailors of the eighteenth century quickly found, the Fisherman's Bend is ideal for mooring smaller boats; it was also then the most popular way of fastening an anchor to a rope (hence the common variation on its name). The knot is strong to the point of being extremely difficult, if not impossible, to untie. It also has the added versatility of being usable in virtually any sort of rope or line, and capable of retaining its stability even when wet, something else that over the centuries cemented its popularity in the maritime world.

HITCHES

HOW TO MAKE A
FISHERMAN'S BEND

The Fisherman's Bend is tied as follows:

STEP 1

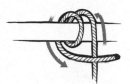

Pass the working end of your line over and around the bar you wish to tether it to. Repeat again so it is wrapped around the bar twice, then place the working end over the standing part.

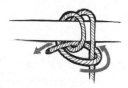

STEP 2

Pass the working end through both of the two turns that go around the bar, completing a Half Hitch.

STEP 3

Bring the working end over the standing part again, then take it around and under the standing part and back over itself, completing a second Half Hitch. Pull to tighten.

PRUSIK KNOT

DIFFICULTY: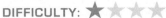

HISTORY

The Prusik Knot is another knot named after its inventor—in this case, the rather eccentric Austrian Dr. Karl Prusik, whose interests and activities, both knot-related and otherwise, were diverse to say the least.

Prusik, born in 1897, was a professor of music engaged in writing a doctoral thesis on lute compositions. He was also an avid mountaineer, serving several times as president of the Austrian Mountaineering Club in the 1930s, during which time he is believed to have pioneered over 70 first ascents on perilous mountain routes. He was also something of a fitness fanatic, going so far as to produce a book entitled *Gymnastik fur Bergsteiger*—an exercise regime aimed specifically at increasing the overall fitness of mountaineers.

It was a combination of these interests that led to Prusik inventing the knot that still bears his name, which he first created during World War I for the purposes of restringing musical instruments. However, Prusik soon realized that there were other applications for the knot, and further developed it over subsequent years. In 1931, it appeared in the *Austrian Mountaineering Journal*, where it was described as an ideal safety knot for use by climbers thanks to the fact that, when tied in a certain way, its loop would provide a hand- or foothold that could easily be slid further up the main line, but which would not slide back when weight was applied by hand or foot.

While his knot and aims toward improving the lot of climbers may have been positive, Prusik's politics seem to have been rather less so. A self-avowed follower of Darwinian philosophy, his attitudes toward physical fitness extended to a belief that exercise was an ideal way to prevent youthful rebellion. He fought in World War I and volunteered for service with the German army in the Second World War. Prusik eventually died in 1961 at the age of 65.

Prusik's name is regularly misspelled, with the knot often errone-ously referred to as a Prussick, Prussic, or Prussik Knot. It is also sometimes called a Triple Sliding Hitch.

BEST USES

The Prusik Knot was long ago displaced from its general use in climbing by more high-tech ascender devices, although it can still be employed in an emergency for the same purpose—namely, ascend-ing a static line—at which times the knot is tied around the rope in question and slid up in stages.

As explained above, the Prusik works well for this particular pur-pose because it provides a loop to grip on to and, while it can be easily slid further up the static line to which it is tied, it will not slide back down. Its use is not limited to mountaineering, however. It can also be used for climbing poles, trees, or similar upright objects, and it is regularly employed by rescue teams the world over.

The Prusik Knot is generally easy to get to grips with and works well on most types of line, although obviously, if it is to be used as a safety device in any kind of potentially dangerous climbing activity, the line needs to be sturdy enough to support the climber in question.

HOW TO MAKE A
PRUSIK KNOT

The Prusik Knot should be tied around the central rope using a sling. If you need to make a sling from a piece of line, then the Fisherman's Bend (see p. 48) is most suitable in this case. Once you have your sling, proceed as follows:

STEP 1

Make a bight in the sling. Place the central rope over this bight, then bend the bight back over the central rope.

STEP 2

Pass the standing part of your sling through its bight, so that it goes over the central rope, then under the bight.

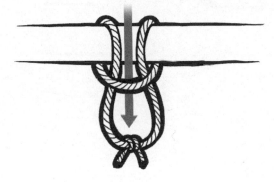

STEP 3

Take the bight and turn it around the central rope again, so that it is now back under the standing part. Pass the standing part back through once more and pull to tighten.

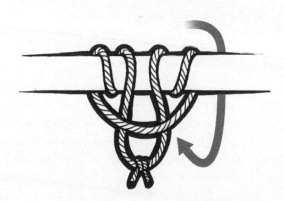

HITCHES

CAMEL HITCH

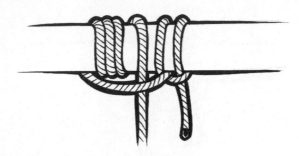

DIFFICULTY: ★ ★ ★ ★

HISTORY

The Camel Hitch may well be the most interestingly-named knot in this book, with certain sources tracing its origins back to the famous nineteenth century Ringling Brothers Circus, where it was used to tie up animals—camels in particular. Its particular suitability for this animal was due to the fact that camels, being ruminants, slobber excessively, and any knot used to tether them becomes rapidly soaked through and thus needs to be resistant to water, which the Camel Hitch certainly is. It is also occasionally known as the Picket Line Hitch, after the structure that animals are frequently tied to.

BEST USES

The Camel Hitch is extremely useful in any number of situations that don't actually involve tying up a live camel. In particular, the knot is regularly employed in the sailing world thanks to the fact that it holds up well when wet and can be pulled on hard from any direction without coming loose. It is also both quick and easy to tie, and can be constructed in lines of various materials and of almost any thickness.

HOW TO MAKE A
CAMEL HITCH

Unlike many knots, the Camel Hitch has just the single variant, tied as follows:

STEP 1

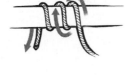

Lay your line over the bar you wish to tie it to. The working end will be the end on the other side of the bar from you. Working from your right, wrap the working end around the bar twice more, taking it In an under-over-under-over pattern.

STEP 2

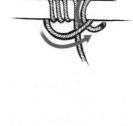

Bring the working end back under the bar, and over the standing part of the line. To the left of the standing part, wrap it round the bar again, going under, then over. As it exits the turn, pass it under itself.

STEP 3

Repeat step two again, taking the line under then over the bar, then back under itself. You should now have two turns round the bar on the right side

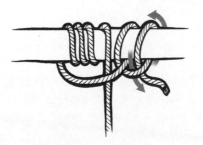

of the line and two on the left. Pull both working end and standing part tight to complete.

HIGHWAYMAN'S HITCH

DIFFICULTY: ★★☆☆

HISTORY

If the Camel Hitch wins the prize for deriving its name from the strangest source, the Highwayman's Hitch probably lays claim to the most romantic—even if there's no actual evidence to back up its peculiar history.

The story behind the knot alleges that it was initially created by highwaymen, who used it to tie their horses to the carriages they were in the process of robbing. Supposedly, the speed with which the knot can be released allowed for a quick getaway, although cynics note that the knot's constitution makes it rather unreliable for tethering horses in the first place. The knot is also known as the Fireman's Hitch.

BEST USES

The Highwayman's Hitch is ideal for tying up any line that needs be released at speed, from a distance, or under conditions in which maneuvering is difficult—hence the highwayman story. However, it is most likely that, by the time the getaway came, the knot would already have capsized, so the Highwayman's Hitch is unreliable when it comes to strength and stability. As such, it isn't suitable for anything that needs to be held too securely.

HOW TO MAKE A HIGHWAYMAN'S HITCH

The Highwayman's Hitch is tied as follows:

STEP 1

With the working end on your left, make a bight in your line. Place it behind the bar you wish to tie it to.

STEP 2

Take the standing part and make a second bight. Lay this over the front of the bar and pass the second bight through the first.

STEP 3

Take the working end and create a third bight in it in front of the bar. Pass this over the first bight and through the second. Hold this third bight and pull the line to tighten.

ROLLING HITCH

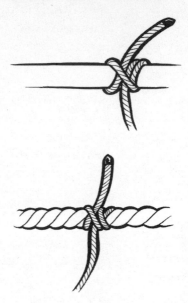

DIFFICULTY: ★ ★ ☆ ☆

HISTORY

The Rolling Hitch's history dates back to the eighteenth century, when—like so many other hitches—it was widely used at sea. However, the knot is unusual in that its name was at the time applied to a different version of the knot than the one we know today.

In the 1700s, the Rolling Hitch was most commonly employed in the rope rigging on ships of the period. However, the knot that was then termed the Rolling Hitch is the one that would later be known as the Two Round Turns or Two Half Hitches; the Rolling Hitch as we know it today was then called either a Magnus Hitch or a Magner's Hitch, a name that some claim it was given in honor of one Mr. Magner, original inventor of the knot.

The first occurrence of the name Rolling Hitch in reference to this knot came in Richard Henry Dana Junior's 1841 book, *The Seaman's Friend*, after which the moniker seemed to stick, although the knot continued to be known by both names for a little while longer, appearing as the Magnus or Magner's Hitch in contemporary works such as *The Young Sea Officer's Anchor* (1808), *The Art of Rigging* (1848), and *Elements and Practice of Rigging and Seamanship* (1794).

Further complicating matters is the fact that, when the knot is tied in such a way that it forms an adjustable loop, it is sometimes referred to as a Taut-Line Hitch. In addition to this, *The Ashley Book of Knots* actually gives two different types of Rolling Hitch, with the Magnus or Magner's Hitch actually listed as an entirely separate knot.

Clifford Ashley's book further implies that the Rolling Hitch is ideal for use in one notable practical joke. It suggests encouraging someone to pull on a rope in which a Rolling Hitch has been tied and then, while they are exerting pressure on it, sliding the knot toward them. This, says Ashley, should have the effect of depositing them on the floor rapidly.

BEST USES

While sharing basic characteristics and strengths, the Rolling Hitch's two variant forms are best used for two entirely separate applications. The first variant should be employed when the line used to tie it is being joined to another line, and the second in cases in which it is being tied to a beam or other solid object.

The Rolling Hitch is known for its ability to withstand strain, and if tied snugly enough, it should not get any tighter under this load. However, the knot is better tied in natural-fiber ropes, since those made of modern synthetic materials will offer less grip and make the knot more likely to slip—indeed, it may be impossible to tie this knot at all with extremely slippery lines. *The Ashley Book of Knots* also suggests that while the version used for attaching two lines together is the more steadfast of the two, the second version is less likely to become twisted.

HOW TO MAKE A ROLLING HITCH

The methods for tying the two different types of Rolling Hitch are described below.

For knots used to tie one line to another line:

STEP 1

Pass the working end over the static line and wrap it around. As it comes out of the turn, bring it over its own standing part.

STEP 2

Repeat again, but pass the working end under itself as it comes out of the turn.

STEP 3

Pull on this and the standing part to tighten.

HITCHES

For knots used to tie a line to a solid bar or similar object:

STEP 1

Pass the working end over the bar. Wrap around the bar, and bring it under its standing part as it comes out of the turn

STEP 2

Pass the working end over the bar again, wrap it around and bring it over its standing part as it comes out of the turn.

STEP 3

Pass the line over the object again, bringing it over itself as it comes out of the turn. Pull the working end and standing part to tighten.

TIMBER/KILLICK HITCH

DIFFICULTY: ★ ★ ★ ☆

HISTORY

Timber and Killick Hitches are further examples of knots dating back several centuries, although the Timber Hitch appears to be the older of the two, originally appearing in the book *A Treatise on Rigging* around 1625. The Killick Hitch, meanwhile, makes its first documented appearance in 1794, when it crops up in David Steel's *Elements and Practice of Rigging and Seamanship*. The word "killick" is itself of maritime origin, referring to a small anchor and thus a nod to the fact that the knot was originally used to secure ships' anchors. The Timber Hitch also takes its name from one of its primary applications—that is, the fastening of ropes to recently-felled timber logs in order to pull them away more easily. The Timber Hitch is also sometimes referred to as the Bowyer's Knot, a reference to the fact that it was at one time used to fasten the bowstring on English longbows.

BEST USES

As previously noted, the Timber Hitch's most popular application is the fastening of lines to felled logs or similar objects to help tow them to another location. The Killick Hitch has similar uses, but it exerts a far harder grip, even when tied to objects with a more slippery finish. That said, both knots are strong, simple to untie, and can be made in almost any type of line.

HITCHES

HOW TO MAKE A TIMBER OR KILLICK HITCH

The two hitches are differentiated only in the final step. They are tied as follows:

STEP 1

Pass the working end of your line behind the bar you wish to tie it to. Bring the working end up and over the bar, so it hangs down in front of the bar.

STEP 2

Pass the working end behind the standing part, then back over both the standing part and itself. Pass the working end back through the turn which goes around the bar. Repeat, so you have an under-over-under pattern, until you have used up all of the working end. Pull on the standing part to tighten the knot.

STEP 3

To convert into a Killick Hitch, tuck the working end through the turn only once. Then, take the working end

behind the bar again, bringing it over the bar so it hangs down in front again. Tuck the working end behind the standing part in front of the bar and pull to tighten.

CHAPTER FOUR
LOOPS

CHAPTER FOUR

LOOPS

DEFINITION

A knot made by doubling a line back on itself to create a loop and then tying the working end to the standing part.

GENERAL PURPOSE AND USES

Loops are generally used in similar instances to hitches, although they can also occasionally take the place of bends; hitches secure a line to an object (usually immovable), while bends join two lines together. A loop can be used in either of these instances, although it differs from the other two knot families in form.

Most loops have their origins in maritime usage, and many are still used in sailing to this day. They are also highly popular among mountaineers and fishermen, the former using them to provide secure foot- and handholds, and the latter to attach hooks and lures to lines. Incidentally, the infamous Hangman's Noose is also a loop—perhaps the most notoriously "useful" loop in history.

The practice of using loops in place of a bend to join ropes involves interlocking two loops; when used in place of a hitch, the loop is placed around a given object and pulled tight. Their various uses have led to many loops being considered among the most important of knots, and as a result they are often some of the first to be taught as a result.

CHARACTERISTICS OF LOOPS

Loops fall into two distinct categories: loops in the end, where the loop is tied in the end of the line, and loops in the bight, where the loop is made in the center of the line. On top of that, there are single, double, and triple loops to contend with—and, as might be expected, single loops are the easiest to tie, although most variations are relatively straightforward to master.

While regularly serving in place of bends or hitches, loops differ in their basic structure from both of these knots. A bend is tied around an object, while a loop is first tied and then placed around the object before being drawn tight. Unlike hitches, loops can be removed from the object they have anchoring, remaining intact where a hitch would almost certainly come untied. Similarly, where a bend requires that the two lines in question be knotted together, loops allow them to be simply tied around each other, rather than to each other, and the fact that they can be loosened and slid up and down the line allows them to be adjusted and reused to secure different objects of various sizes.

LOOPS

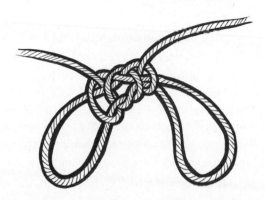

OVERHAND LOOP

LOOPS

DIFFICULTY: ★ ☆ ☆ ☆

HISTORY

The Overhand Loop is derived from the Overhand Knot, although details of its invention appear not to have been recorded, most likely because it is one of the most basic and obvious of knots. It has also occasionally been known throughout history as the Loop Fish Knot or simply the Loop Knot, and may well have its origins in the fishing world, where it is used to this day for attaching hooks to lines.

BEST USES

The Overhand Loop is probably the easiest of all loops to tie, but it is not necessarily the strongest: while reasonably secure in natural fiber line, it is less stable in synthetic materials, although it can be tied in virtually any type of line. It is also one of the more difficult loops to untie from any material, especially if it has become wet or been placed under excessive strain. As previously mentioned, it is most commonly used to tie fishing hooks to lines, although it is also regularly employed to tie down loads on trucks or wagons. The Double Overhand Loop, also described on the next page, suffers from many of the same flaws, but it is slightly stronger.

HOW TO MAKE AN OVERHAND LOOP

An Overhand Loop is tied in the bight as follows:

STEP 1

Starting with the working end of your line pointing toward your left, bring the end down and round to form a bight. Taking hold of the bight so you are working with a doubled line, bring it down, then up and over the standing part to form a loop.

STEP 2

Pass the bight through the loop, going first under, then over, and pull to tighten.

STEP 3

To create a Double Overhand Loop, use a longer bight. Make the knot as above, but when passing the bight through the loop, take it over and under, and repeat again before pulling tight.

BOWLINE

LOOPS

DIFFICULTY: ★ ★ ★ ★

HISTORY

The Bowline makes its first appearance in the 1627 book *Seaman's Grammar* by John Smith, although it may well date back much further than this. Some believe that it may even have been used in ancient Egypt, as a knot closely resembling it was discovered in the tomb of the pharaoh Cheops.

Either way, the knot was well established by the seventeenth and eighteenth centuries, making two subsequent appearances in books of this period: *The Seaman's Dictionary* (1644) and *Elements and Practice of Rigging and Seamanship* (1794). Both refer to the knot as being primarily used for tying forward a square sail's weather leech; in layman's terms, this means preventing the sail from being accidentally blown inside out by the wind by tying a line from the sail to the ship's bow, and it was from this same practice that the knot took its name—initially a Bow Line Knot, now a Bowline, but pronounced "boh-lynn."

BEST USES

There are numerous "loop in the end" knots, all of them capable of being tied around a post, bollard, or similar object, but the Bowline is unique among its peers thanks to its potential for being passed around the object in question prior to being tied. As such, tying two Bowlines can be a good way of joining a pair of lines together or fixing a line that has snapped—although it should be borne in mind when doing so that there are other, stronger methods for joining lines.

Primarily, the Bowline remains mostly frequently used on board sailing ships, where it can be employed for any purpose that requires a single loop knot. It is also a popular addition to safety harnesses, tied around the waists of sailors for support when working over the side of a vessel, or by climbers as a back-up system to their regular climbing harnesses.

Even after it has been subjected to heavy stress, the Bowline remains easy to untie—a fact greatly adding to its usefulness as a support knot—although it is remarkably strong while tied. That said, if the load placed upon it is varied over time, or the line itself is jerked repeatedly, it can become loosened. It is easy and quick to tie, can be learned rapidly and is well suited to most types of line.

HOW TO MAKE A BOWLINE

As one of the most useful and easy knots to tie, the Bowline is under-standably also one of the first that many learn (along with the Overhand and Figure-Eight Knots, both listed in the section on stopper knots). The knot features the same basic structure as the Sheet Bend, and is tied in the end of the line as follows:

STEP 1

Bring the working end over the stand-ing part to form an overhand loop. Take hold of the loop and move it clockwise, so that it comes up and over both the standing part and work-ing end. This will create a second, smaller loop.

STEP 2

Pass the working end through the loop. Take it round under the standing part of the line.

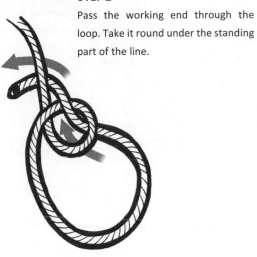

STEP 3

Bring the working end back to the front and feed it through the second loop, going first over, then under. Take hold of the working end and standing part and pull to tighten.

ANGLER'S LOOP

DIFFICULTY: ★ ★ ☆ ☆

LOOPS

HISTORY

The Angler's Loop is believed by some to date back as far as the seventeenth century, when it is thought to have been invented by Izaak Walton, author of *The Compleat Angler*, although this has never been conclusively proved. What is known is that the knot has been mistakenly labelled as a Blood Loop in the past, and is occasionally referred to as a Perfection Loop.

BEST USES

The Angler's Loop is considered to be a good loop for general use in a wide variety of applications. It is simple to learn and easily tied at speed, although its tendency to jam in natural-fiber ropes led to it falling out of favor with sailors in the past—a problem largely rectified by the proliferation of modern synthetic lines.

The knot is strong and secure, although once pulled tight it is extremely difficult—if not impossible—to untie, often necessitating cutting the line. As such, it should only be used when a permanent knot is required. It can be tied in both thick lines and in flexible cable such as bungee cords.

HOW TO MAKE AN ANGLER'S LOOP

The Angler's Loop is made in the end of the line as follows:

STEP 1

With the working end of your line, make an underhand loop. Bring the working end back over the loop so that it lies across the top.

STEP 2

Take hold of the line where it crosses the loop and pull it through, thus creating a draw-loop.

STEP 3

Take the working end and pass it under the standing part before bringing it up and passing it through the knot in an over-under-under-over pattern, which will take it over the initial loop and under the draw-loop. Pull the working end and standing part to tighten.

FIREMAN'S CHAIR KNOT

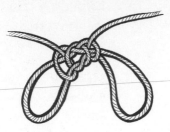

DIFFICULTY: ★★☆☆

HISTORY

The Fireman's Chair Knot has been used for centuries to create slings to support people being lowered from great heights in emergency situations, or to aid climbers attempting various descents. It clearly predates the safer, more modern harnesses that are, these days, used in its place, although details of its exact origins have never been recorded. It has also been known by a string of variant names throughout history, including the Chair Knot, Fireman's Knot, Hitched Tom Fool's Knot, and Man-Harness from Tom Fool's Knot.

BEST USES

This particular loop is nowadays most widely used to maneuver rescue victims in emergency situations where no safety harness is available. It is a double-loop knot, and, when used to move an accident victim or other person, one loop should be passed under the armpits to support the body while the other goes beneath the knees. Pulling these loops snug to the body should allow the manipulation of even unconscious people with only minimal risk or danger of falling. The knot is suitable for use with most types of line (although any being used to support a person's weight should obviously be strong), and it is easily learned and quick to tie. It also benefits from being easily adjustable, allowing the person in the harness it creates to be freed from its grip rapidly when desired. Its basic structure strongly resembles that of the Handcuff Knot.

HOW TO MAKE A
FIREMAN'S CHAIR KNOT

When tying this knot, it is important to do so centrally in a line of length equal to or greater than twice the height of the person being lowered. It should also be noted that this knot should only be used as a last resort:

STEP 1

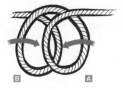

Create a bight in the center of your line. Twist it toward your right to create a loop (Loop A). Create a second bight to the left of the first and twist it toward your right to create a second loop of similar size next to the first (Loop B).

STEP 2

Move the two loops toward each other, bringing Loop A over Loop B overlapping. Pull the left edge of Loop A under the left edge of Loop B, and the right edge of Loop B over the right edge of Loop A. Pull both simultaneously to make tight.

STEP 3

Take the working end of the line that is to your left, bringing it first under, then over the newly-formed loop on the left, then back under itself. Take the working end on your right and pass it first over, then under the newly formed loop on your right, and finally back over itself. Pull both newly-formed loops to tighten.

ENGLISHMAN'S LOOP

DIFFICULTY: ★★☆☆

HISTORY

Also known as the Fisherman's Loop or Angler's Loop, this particular knot has its origins—unsurprisingly—in angling and was first conceived in the days when fishing lines were made of gut, being its strongest when tied in such lines. The knot has also been variously known throughout history as the Cove Knot, Middleman's Knot, and Waterman's Knot and is also one of a number of knots to have been referred to as the True Lover's Knot.

BEST USES

The Englishman's Loop is a strong knot that works well with modern synthetic ropes and similar lines, but struggles when tied in particularly shiny-surfaced material such as nylon. It once enjoyed a degree of popularity among the climbing community, but has since fallen out of favor and been replaced by knots like the Alpine Butterfly (below). Large and bulky, the Englishman's Loop is fairly easy to tie but often difficult to untie.

HOW TO MAKE AN ENGLISHMAN'S LOOP

The Englishman's Loop is tied in the end of the line as follows:

STEP 1

Make an Overhand Knot in your line by making an overhand loop with the working end and then taking it in through the loop and under, then over. Bring the working end round again and pass it back through the loop of the Overhand Knot, going first over, then under.

STEP 2

Behind the initial Overhand Knot (i.e., on the opposite side of the loop), create a second Overhand Knot. Do this by making an overhand loop with the working end. This should go under the standing part, then back over both the standing part and the working end. Take the working end through the loop, going first under then over to complete the Overhand Knot.

STEP 3

Take hold of your loop and hold the standing part and working end together, then pull tight to finish.

ALPINE BUTTERFLY KNOT

DIFFICULTY: ★ ★ ★ ★

HISTORY

Believed to originate in Europe, the Alpine Butterfly Knot is thought to have been invented by mountaineers at least a century ago, and it is also occasionally known as the Lineman's Loop, the Butterfly Loop, or the Alpine Butterfly Loop—although the "Alpine" part of the title is a more recent addition, dating back just 30 years or so.

BEST USES

As previously mentioned, the Alpine Butterfly Knot's primary use remains in mountaineering, where it is most often employed by climbers to attach themselves to the center of a rope. Its suitability for this purpose is derived from the fact that it retains its extraordinary strength when pulled in various directions, and can thus be trusted with a climber's suspended weight even when he or she is moving around erratically. The knot can also act as a bend for the emergency reattachment of broken rope ends. While not the easiest of knots to tie, the Alpine Butterfly does have the advantage of being suitable for almost any type of line, and it is easy to untie unless it becomes wet.

HOW TO MAKE AN ALPINE BUTTERFLY KNOT

The Alpine Butterfly is made in the bight as follows:

STEP 1

Take your line and make an overhand loop at the point where you wish to tie the knot. Taking hold of the top of the loop, twist it toward the right so that it looks like a figure eight.

STEP 2

Taking the top of the upper loop, fold it down behind the line, enlarging it as you go.

STEP 3

Taking the center of the upper loop, fold it up over the line and pass it up through the smaller loop. Pull to tighten.

FIGURE-EIGHT LOOP

DIFFICULTY: ★★★★

HISTORY

Originating in climbing circles, the Figure-Eight Loop was rapidly adopted by seafarers thanks to its relative ease of tying in comparison with the Bowline, especially in adverse weather conditions. Its popularity among mountaineers derives from similar reasons, not to mention the fact that it is secure, very strong, and easy to double check. The knot is also occasionally known as the Double Figure Eight, Figure Eight on the Bight, Guide Knot, and the Flemish Loop.

BEST USES

Still widely used both in the mountains and at sea, the Figure Eight Loop has also found applications in camping and caving. It is a fairly versatile knot in that it can be tied in the center of a rope or in one that has been doubled over, as well as being reliable where the line is slippery. It is also easy to learn, can be tied very quickly, and is famously strong and secure. On the downside, excessive pressure exerted on the rope can cause the knot to jam, making it subsequently difficult to untie, plus the Figure Eight Loop is rather large and bulky, meaning that it won't pass through an eye or similar circlet.

LOOPS

HOW TO MAKE A FIGURE-EIGHT LOOP

The Figure-Eight Loop is tied in the bight as follows:

STEP 1

Take hold of your line in the center and bring the working end round to create a bight. Hold the bight so that you are now working with a doubled line.

STEP 2

Bring your doubled line back under its standing part, then over the standing part, thus creating the two-loop "figure eight."

STEP 3

Bring the bight through the upper loop of the eight, going first under, then over. Take hold of the bight and the standing part and pull to tighten.

CHAPTER FIVE
SLIP KNOTS

CHAPTER FIVE

SLIP KNOTS

Definition

Slip knots, also known as running knots, break down into two distinct categories: in the first are those knots used to fasten a line to a particular object, and which tighten when a load is placed on the end; in the second are those knots that fasten one line to the center of another line, and which then allow the knot to slide along this line either in one direction or both directions.

General Purpose and Uses

The two varieties of slip knot are used in different ways. Slip knots that are designed to tighten when their line is tied to an object have been most widely employed for less than pleasant purposes, most notably throughout history—indeed, in some parts of the world to this day—as a method of execution thanks to the infamous Hangman's Noose. Similarly, automatically tightening knots are used in snares to trap animals, although one more day-to-day usage is the mooring of boats, particularly in conditions where the tide may rise or fall, or where the boat may be subject to currents that place irregular stress on the line, causing it to become more secure in the process.

The other variety of slip knot, in which the knot can move up or down a second line to which it has been tied, is most widely used in mountaineering. Originally, these knots provided a means for climbing up ropes safely, but, with the onset of modern technology, they are now mostly used as back-up safety devices.

Characteristics of a Slip Knot

Since slip knots are used to tie objects to lines or to fasten ropes together, they are also technically hitches; while every hitch is not a slip knot, all hitches can be converted into slip knots by tying them around the standing part of their lines, and some hitches are slip knots by default. Both the Clove Hitch and Rolling Hitch, featured in the hitch section of this book, are also slip knots.

The second variety of slip knot—those that move along a rope to which the line has been attached—generally all feature a large loop, usually used to gain a foot- or handhold in climbing. As this loop does not usually go around either an object or the second rope, however, these knots are not considered members of the loop family.

THE SLIP KNOT

DIFFICULTY: ★ ☆ ☆ ☆

HISTORY

Another knot seemingly named for the purposes of causing confusion. The fact that this is the simplest of all slip knots is presumably the reason it is referred to as the Slip Knot, as well as being a member of the slip knot family. It does go by other names, however, including the Noose, the Running Knot, and the Single Bow, and it has been around in some form or other for centuries.

BEST USES

The Slip Knot has a variety of diverse uses. In the countryside, it has been used widely in the creation of basic snares for catching birds, rabbits, or other small creatures, while in the home it is another of the knots most often used to tie packages. In climbing, it can be used to create a tie-off point, or to attach gear to a line. While fairly secure, it should not be used in situations where it is expected to support a person's weight, as it may not be strong enough for this purpose. The knot is very easy and quick to tie and is adaptable to almost any material. It can also be rapidly unraveled by simply pulling on one end of the rope—and as such it is ideal for use in temporary applications.

HOW TO MAKE
A SLIP KNOT

The basic Slip Knot is tied as follows:

STEP 1

Taking the working end on your left, make a counterclockwise underhand loop.

STEP 2

Move the loop toward your right, and place it over the standing part of the line.

STEP 3

Grip the standing part where it passes under the loop and lead it upward through the loop. Pull to tighten.

RUNNING BOWLINE

DIFFICULTY: ★★★★

HISTORY

The Running Bowline's history follows that of the Bowline itself, since—as its name suggests—it is a variant of that same knot and is pronounced similarly ("Running Boh-Lynn"). This presumably means that the Running Bowline could well date back just as far, reaching a peak in its popularity among sailors of the seventeenth and eighteenth centuries. Structurally, it is virtually the same as the Bowline but for the simple addition of tying the loop around the standing part of the line in which the knot itself has been made.

BEST USES

While this knot's basic structure and name may recall the standard Bowline, the fact that it is in fact a slip knot means that it is most useful under completely different circumstances. While the Bowline is used to anchor sails and the like, the Running Bowline can be utilized for a variety of purposes—as a noose to hoist large weighty sacks, for example, or in the production of animal snares. Its loop can also be lowered into deep holes or bodies of water to recover lost objects—a purpose to which it lends itself well thanks to the fact that the knot is secure only under tension, in this case provided by the object being retrieved. The knot is also relatively easy to tie and can be fashioned in any type of material.

HOW TO MAKE A
RUNNING BOWLINE

The Running Bowline is constructed in a similar fashion to the standard Bowline, with only minor alterations, as follows:

STEP 1

Bring the working end of your line back against the standing part to form a bight, with the working end to your left. In the working end, make a counterclockwise overhand loop, then pass the working end under the standing part.

STEP 2

Bring the working end back over the standing part, then through the loop, going first under, then over.

STEP 3

Beneath the loop, pass the working end under itself, then back through the loop, going first over, then under. Pull the working end to tighten.

TARBUCK KNOT

DIFFICULTY: ★ ★ ☆ ☆

HISTORY

Like the Prusik Knot, the Tarbuck Knot was named after its inventor, although it was devised some 20 years after the Prusik and for entirely different reasons. Ken Tarbuck, a noted skier and climber, invented his own contribution to the knotting world in 1952 as a reaction to the proliferation of synthetic nylon ropes, which rendered many older climbing knots redundant through slippage. Tarbuck wanted a knot that could be used for the express purpose of making safe a sudden stress—for example, a falling body on the end of the line—even in the notoriously slippery nylon ropes. The Tarbuck Knot achieves exactly this by slipping to an extent, then holding as the pressure is reduced to a safe level.

BEST USES

Unfortunately for Tarbuck, his namesake knot became almost immediately redundant for its designated purpose thanks to the invention of kernmantel ropes, which could absorb sudden loads through their own elasticity, and which could be ruined by the untimely application of a Tarbuck Knot. However, the knot can still be utilized as a general slide and grip loop knot since, like the Prusik, it can be moved along by hand, and will lock under load. It is nowadays perhaps most widely used to pitch tents and to temporarily tether smaller boats in places where the tide will be going in or out. It is also extremely easy to untie.

HOW TO MAKE A
TARBUCK KNOT

The Tarbuck Knot is fairly easy to tie, the trickier part coming toward the end of the tying process. It is created as follows:

STEP 1

Take the working end of your line and make a clockwise overhand loop. Pass the working end back into the loop, taking it under the lower edge of the loop. Take it back over the lower edge of the loop to complete one turn.

STEP 2

Continue to take the working end in an under-over pattern to form a second turn about the lower edge of the loop.

STEP 3

As the working end exits the loop, bring it up outside the loop and round under the standing part of the line. Tuck it back over, then under itself and carefully remove the slack.

CHAPTER SIX
SPLICES

CHAPTER SIX

SPLICES

DEFINITION OF A SPLICE
A splice is a join made between two lines (usually ropes), or between two ends of the same rope, by unlacing the ropes' various threads and then weaving those threads together.

GENERAL PURPOSE AND USES
Rope splicing is most widely used at sea and has been for centuries. The practice is employed for three main reasons: to join ropes together in order to increase their length; to join the ends of one line to form a sling; and to repair a line which has been severed, snapped, or otherwise worn through. Splices are also occasionally used to "seal off" the end of a line and thus prevent it from fraying.

Splicing two lines together has the advantage of being more secure than simply knotting them—even the strongest knot decreases a given line's strength by 40%, while weaker knots can lessen a line's integrity even further. While not quite as strong as an unbroken line, a spliced rope retains up to 95% of its original strength, depending on which method is used. The only downside is that this usually results in a thickening of the line at the point where it is spliced, making it cumbersome to use under some circumstances.

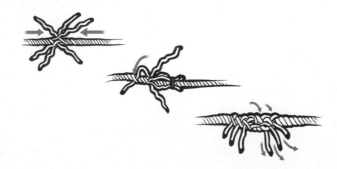

CHARACTERISTICS OF A SPLICE

Simply put, splices require that the rope ends being joined have their strands unpicked to a pre-determined length before being interwoven to join the two ropes—a completely different action to regular knotting that sets splices apart from bends. For obvious reasons, splicing can only be used on lines made of braided threads: three-strand rope is the most suitable, although the practice can be applied to ropes braided from 12 strands or even more. As already mentioned, splicing does have the often unwanted effect of thickening the line at the splicing point, although this can be reduced, if not completely eradicated, by tapering the strands to meld them more smoothly into the line.

Splices are semipermanent. They can be unpicked if necessary, but this will damage the rope in question by splaying the formerly spliced strands, which will then need to be trimmed off.

Unlike other types of knot, splicing sometimes requires the use of particular tools, as not all rope lines are so easily unpicked; the marlinespike and fid can be especially helpful in unpicking and then splicing the strands of particularly new or stiff ropes.

EYE SPLICE

DIFFICULTY: ★ ★ ☆ ☆

HISTORY

Like all splices, the Eye Splice has its origins in the maritime world. Its name derives from the loop or "eye" formed by splicing the working end of the line into the standing part; in its earliest incarnations, it was stated that the end of each strand should be tucked back just three times, although more modern variations suggest a minimum of five.

BEST USES

The Eye Splice is the best type of splicing to use with three-stranded rope, for which it is the most efficient way of forming a loop in the end of the line. The difference between the number of suggested tucks in earlier and later directions is down to a variation in materials used. With older, natural-fiber lines, three tucks would have been sufficient to make a strong splice, but more modern synthetic lines require the suggested five tucks before being strong enough to hold—although even more should be used if the line is to hold anything particularly heavy. While not especially difficult, this splice does require some care and practice to get right.

HOW TO MAKE AN EYE SPLICE

When making an Eye Splice, the ends of the line should be either bound with tape or flame-treated in order to stop them from becoming overly frayed. The splice is made as follows:

STEP 1

Unlay the line to a point about seven turns into the rope. Gauging how large an eye you wish to create, pass one of the strands under a strand in the standing part of the rope.

STEP 2

Take hold of your second strand, and tuck this one under the strand beneath the one you joined with the first loose strand.

STEP 3

Turning the rope around, pass your third loose strand under the strand between the two already used in the standing part. Repeat this process five times and trim any leftover ends from the loose strands.

SPLICES

SHORT SPLICE

DIFFICULTY: ★★★☆

HISTORY

The Short Splice method results in an extremely strong join—although the downside of this is that the spliced section will be roughly twice the thickness of the rest of the line.

BEST USES

The Short Splice can either be used to join two ends of the same piece of rope to form a sling or to meld together two entirely separate lines. It has various advantages: being relatively easy to learn, quick to carry out, and consuming far less rope than other splices. As already noted, the Short Splice is also far stronger than any knot used for the same purpose, but the accompanying increase in diameter means that it cannot be used in any situation in which the line is expected to pass through a small eye or hole.

HOW TO MAKE A SHORT SPLICE

A short splicex involves "marrying" together the ends of two lines as follows:

STEP 1

Unlay your two lines, Rope A and Rope B, going up about seven turns into each. Place the two ends together so that each loose strand is between two loose strands belonging to the other rope.

STEP 2

Temporarily anchor the strands of Rope B to Rope A by tying a piece of string around them. Take hold of one of the loose strands of Rope A and pass it over one of the loose strands of Rope B, then under the next. Repeat with the other two loose strands of Rope A and continue weaving the two ropes together in this manner.

STEP 3

Remove the temporary anchoring from Rope B's loose strands. Take one loose strand and pass it over one of the formerly loose strands of Rope A, then under the next. Repeat with the next two loose strands of Rope B and continue in the same manner as step 2 until Rope B is fully interwoven with Rope A.

BACK SPLICE

DIFFICULTY: ★ ★ ★ ★

HISTORY

Another naval invention, the Back Splice is also occasionally referred to as the End Splice, a name deriving from the way in which the rope strands are spliced straight back into the end of the line without forming a loop. The splice has also been periodically known as a Crown Splice (as the strands are effectively tied into a Crown Knot before being spliced back into the line), a Spanish Whipping and, more obscurely, a Dog Pointing. The Back Splice is also used for decorative purposes.

BEST USES

For many years, the Back Splice was most widely employed in the rope-making industry to finish off the end of a line and prevent any unwanted fraying or unraveling, although the prevalence of heat sealing in the production of modern synthetic lines—in which strands are simply melted and fused together—has largely rendered this practice obsolete.

The Back Splice does still have its uses, however. Like the Short Splice, it thickens the line used to make it, and when used to finish off the end of a rope this allows the end to be found by touch alone in situations where visibility is less than perfect. It is also quick and relatively easy to carry out, and as such is useful in emergencies or when time is otherwise of the essence.

HOW TO MAKE A
BACK SPLICE

As with the other splices, you will need to begin by unlaying your rope's strands up to about seven turns into the line. Then proceed as follows:

STEP 1

Taking your three separate strands, loop the rightmost strand over to form a bight. Place the middle strand over this bight. Bring the leftmost strand under the first strand then over the second. Next, bring it through the bight, going under, then over the line.

STEP 2

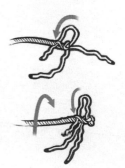

Pull the three strands tight, which will effectively tie them in a Crown Knot. Taking one loose strand, pass it under the second of the strands still braided together just beneath your knot. Turning the rope 120 degrees, repeat for the second of your loose strands, then turn again, and repeat for the third.

STEP 3

Being sure to keep the splice as tight as you can, continue in this manner, passing the loose strands under every second of the still-braided strands, until all length in the loose strands has been used up. If you have leftover length in any of the loose strands, you can trim this, although be sure not to trim too close to the rope, as this can cause the splice to unravel.

CHAPTER SEVEN
STOPPER KNOTS

CHAPTER SEVEN

STOPPER KNOTS

Definition of a Stopper Knot

A knot tied in a line either to prevent that line from unraveling or to stop it from passing through a small opening.

General Purpose and Uses

Stopper knots originated at sea and remain widely employed in the rigging of sails today, although they can also be found in guylines for the pitching of tents and in various creative pursuits such as macramé and Chinese rope design. The knots are also tied into the ends of multistrand ropes to insure against unwanted fraying or unraveling—a purpose to which they are suited even when tied into thinner, more everyday lines such as thread, string, and other household materials.

In addition, stopper knots can be used to create handholds or footholds in cases where ropes are being used for climbing purposes. Their suitability in these circumstances was first discovered aboard ships, where they were tied using the strands of unravelled rope (the rope then being rewoven above the knot) and used to ascend masts and rigging.

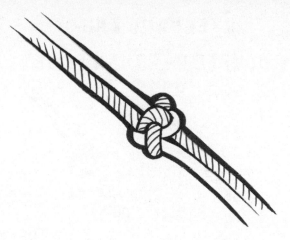

Characteristics of a
Stopper Knot

The nature of their applications tends to demand stopper knots be fairly bulky, although their size does vary dramatically. Most are semipermanent, strong, and fairly stable, but can be easily untied, although some will seize up under strain and require cutting off, and others can be undone only when tied in a thicker cord or kept dry. The majority of stopper knots are tied in the end of a line, although there are certain exceptions to this rule that are tied in the bight.

Structurally, stopper knots can be divided into two categories: single-strand knots and multistrand knots. Single-strand knots are those tied using just one piece of line, while multistrand knots are those tied using the unpicked strands of lines usually composed of three or four strands; they become less effective when tied in lines made up of more strands than this.

OVERHAND KNOT/ DOUBLE OVERHAND KNOT

DIFFICULTY: ★ ☆ ☆ ☆

HISTORY

The Overhand Knot is the most basic form of stopper knot—indeed, one of the most basic of all knots. Its structure forms the foundation of countless other knots including the Angler's Loop, the Blood Knot, and the Fisherman's Knot. It is, in fact, the knot that ropes, pieces of string, and other lines left tangled up and lying around can be virtually counted on to tie themselves into—a fact that suggests it is also one of the oldest knots on earth.

BEST USES

As well as being a stopper knot, the Overhand Knot is often used to make lines easier to grip by being tied at regular intervals to form a makeshift handrail; it is also occasionally used for purely decorative purposes. As a stopper knot, meanwhile, it is extremely versatile in terms of materials, capable of being tied into everything from thick rope to the thinnest of thread. That said, the simplicity of its structure belies its great strength: after being subjected to strain the knot can be virtually impossible to untie, especially in thinner lines or rope that has been exposed to water; the Double Overhand Knot, which adds a further pass to the original version, is even harder to unpick.

HOW TO MAKE AN OVERHAND AND DOUBLE OVERHAND KNOT

Both knots are tied in the end of the line as follows:

STEP 1

Bring the working end downward and then up to form an overhand loop.

STEP 2

Pass the working end back through the loop, going first under, then over, and pull to tighten.

To convert this into a Double Overhand Knot, add the following step before pulling to tighten:

STEP 3

Bring the working end over, then under, then over the loop again. Pull to tighten.

STOPPER KNOTS

STEVEDORE'S KNOT

DIFFICULTY: ★ ★ ★ ★

HISTORY

The Stevedore's Knot derives its name from the longshoremen who originally developed it for the purposes of unloading cargo off boats one piece at a time, long before the invention of mechanized cranes. For this they would use a manual hoist to lift crates, sacks, and the like into and out of a ship's hold, but to ensure that the rope didn't slip through the hoist pulley, they needed a stopper knot that would be strong and bulky yet easy to untie after being subjected to great strain—and thus the Stevedore's Knot was born. It is also sometimes called the Figure Nine Knot due to its shape.

BEST USES

The loading and unloading of commercial cargo became automated long ago, but single rope pulleys remain in use all over the world, and the Stevedore's Knot is still an excellent way of ensuring that no line ever slips through such a device. Not all of its applications are quite so industrial, however: the knot is also considered by many to be the perfect stopper for suspending conkers from a thread or stringing beads. It can be tied in most types of line and works well with thick rope, is also easy to learn, quick to tie, and simple to take out of all but the finest line.

HOW TO MAKE A STEVEDORE'S KNOT

The Stevedore's Knot is tied in the bight as follows:

STEP 1

Make an overhand loop with one working end of your line. Taking hold of the loop, twist it upward to form a figure eight shape.

STEP 2

Repeat the twist twice more, so that the line crosses itself a total of four times.

STEP 3

Take the working end and bring it up through the end of the loop, going first under, then over, and pull to tighten.

FIGURE-EIGHT KNOT

DIFFICULTY: ★ ★ ☆ ☆

HISTORY

Still the most frequently used stopper knot more than 200 years since it was first invented, the hugely versatile Figure-Eight Knot originated at sea during the nineteenth century. It was first identified by this name in 1808, when it was recorded as a noted method for holding down sheet sails in Darcy Lever's book, *The Young Officer's Sheet Anchor*, although at the time it was also sometimes known as the Flemish Knot. Much later, the knot had the honor of being recommended by the highly influential Surrey, England, branch of the International Guild of Knot Tyers as the first knot any aspiring enthusiast should learn to make in a line.

BEST USES

Like many stopper knots, the Figure-Eight Knot shares a degree of cross-pollination with knots from various other families, and can be easily altered to create a bend, hitch, or loop. It is equally versatile in its role as a stopper knot, applicable in any situation in which a line needs to pass through a hole without running all the way through and escaping. As quick and simple to tie as it is to untie, the Figure Eight is also fairly stable, although it is known to come undone if subjected to continuous oscillatory movements.

HOW TO MAKE A FIGURE-EIGHT KNOT

This is a single-strand stopper knot, tied in the end of the line as follows:

STEP 1

Take the working end of your line and make an overhand loop. Take hold of the loop and twist upward, forming the figure eight shape.

STEP 2

Take the working end round from behind the standing part and pass through the first loop (now the "top" loop of the figure eight), going first over, then under.

STEP 3

Pull the working end and standing part to tighten.

ASHLEY'S STOPPER KNOT

DIFFICULTY: ★★☆☆

HISTORY

Ashley's Stopper Knot is named after the American Clifford Ashley, the man who discovered it; as the author of *The Ashley Book of Knots* (1944), its namesake is also one of the most important figures in knotting history.

Born in New Bedford, Massachusetts, in 1881, Ashley attended the Eric Pape School of Art in Boston, where he studied under the landscape painter George Noyes before setting himself up as a commercial artist and writer. A keen sailor, much of Ashley's work at the time was published in *Harper's* magazine, including various articles on whaling that he later compiled into a book on the subject.

It was while working for *Harper's* that Ashley first stumbled upon the knot that would later come to bear his name. It was around 1910, and Ashley was on a boat named the *Mattie Flavel* in the Delaware Bay region, where he had been commissioned to produce a number of illustrations depicting the local oyster fishing industry. It was here that Ashley spotted a boat with an unusual knot tied into its rigging. Thinking it too large to be a Figure-Eight Knot, Ashley asked the sailors on his own ship to tell him its name, but none could. By this point the boat in question had overtaken them, meaning that Ashley was forced to attempt the knot from memory alone—the result of which he named the Oysterman's Knot. Several days later, however, Ashley saw the mysterious boat again, this time moored, and was thus able to board and investigate himself. The knot turned out to be nothing more than a Figure-Eight Knot that had become enlarged due to repeated soakings; his own Oysterman's Knot, however, was something entirely different.

This event led to a sharp increase in Ashley's own interest in knots, and thus to the eventual publication of his book, which categorized more than 3,800 knots, featuring illustrations and detailed instructions for each. Ashley himself suffered a stroke the year following its publication and died in 1947, but *The Ashley Book of Knots*—widely considered to be the knot enthusiast's bible—remains in print to this day.

BEST USES

The extremely bulky Ashley's Stopper Knot is generally used for all the same purposes as the popular Figure-Eight Knot, but takes precedence in instances where the Figure Eight is too small to prevent the line in question from escaping from whatever hole it is passing through. As such, it has many applications in sailing, as well as in the practice of pitching tents. The Ashley's Stopper Knot is relatively easy to learn and simple to tie and untie, but its size makes it better suited to heavier lines and less practical for use with thinner materials.

HOW TO MAKE AN
ASHLEY'S STOPPER KNOT

Ashley's Stopper Knot is tied in the
end, as follows:

STEP 1

Bring the working end of your line
down, then under the standing part
to form an underhand loop. Move
this loop upward and place it so it
overlaps the standing part of the line.

STEP 2

Taking hold of the standing part where it passes under the loop, pull this up and through the loop, giving a draw-loop.

STEP 3

Take hold of the working end of the line, and pass this through the draw-loop in an under-over pattern. Pull both the working end and standing part of the line to tighten.

STOPPER KNOTS

CROWN KNOT

DIFFICULTY: ★ ★ ★ ☆

HISTORY

The Crown Knot has been dated back to at least the eighteenth century, and is notable for the fact that it is the exact reverse of the Wall Knot—an upside-down Wall Knot is a Crown Knot, and vice versa. Also notable is the fact that, like the Wall Knot, the Crown is infrequently used by itself, but forms the basis of numerous more complex knots of different varieties—most commonly the Back Splice. Like many knots of the period, it most likely originated onboard ships.

BEST USES

The Crown Knot is highly decorative and often finds employment in various artistic pursuits, but it is of little practical use in and of itself. It is, however, widely used as a basis for more complex ropework; as well as the Back Splice, it also provides the structural foundation for Sennits and other lanyard knots. Combined with its reverse, the Wall Knot, it becomes a component of the appropriately named Wall and Crown Knot. It is generally tied with unpicked strands of rope like a splice, and as such is most commonly tied in three-strand line, although it can be made in line with a higher number of strands. The knot is solid and stable, and is fairly easy to learn and quick to tie.

HOW TO MAKE A CROWN KNOT

This multistrand stopper knot is tied in three-strand line as follows:

STEP 1

Take the three strands of your line and form an overhand loop in each of the first two. Pass the working end of the first line through the loop of the second, going first over, then under. Pass the working end of the second over the third.

STEP 2

Bring the working end of the third strand over the working end of the second and through the loop of the first, going first over, then under. Pull to tighten.

STEP 3

To make a Wall Knot, follow the instructions above, but take each line under and then over when passing through the loops.

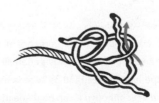

DIAMOND KNOT

DIFFICULTY: ★ ★ ★ ★

HISTORY

Variously known as the Lanyard Knot and the Chinese Button Knot, the Diamond Knot has been in use for centuries. It is believed to have had its origins at sea, although it differs from many other nautical knots in that its purpose was often purely decorative. The Diamond moniker comes from its ornate shape, although the name Lanyard Knot is derived from the cords tied around the neck or waist, from which tools and other useful items were suspended tools. Sailors would decorate these lanyards with aesthetically pleasing knots, of which this was one of the most popular.

BEST USES

While mostly used for decorative purposes, the Diamond Knot can still function as a stopper knot. It is usually tied in the standing part of a line using the unpicked strands of a rope, which are then rewoven together when they emerge from the knot. It can be tied with three- or four-strand line, and can be somewhat tricky to master initially. Once tied, it is strong and fairly permanent.

HOW TO MAKE A
DIAMOND KNOT

While it is often tied as a multistrand stopper knot, the simplest method of tying the Diamond Knot is in a single-strand line as follows:

STEP 1

Taking a length of cord, make a counterclockwise underhand loop in the working end to your right (End A). End A should now point straight downward. Take the working end to your left (End B) and pass it under End A, and under the loop. This should form a second loop to the left of the first one.

STEP 2

In the shape you have now, End A should pass through the center of the second loop. Pass End B back through the second loop and under End A. This should give you an over-under-over pattern as End B passes through the loop. This will form a third loop.

STEP 3

Next, pass End B through the first of the three loops. This should be the one on your right-hand side. Take it over the lower edge, under the line bisecting the loop, then over the uppermost edge.

STEP 4

Take End A and bring it up to your right. Then pass it back down under the uppermost edge of the first-formed loop, and under the two lines that cross in the center of the loop. Bringing End A to the center of the knot, take it up and over both the two lines crossing in the oppo-site loop and the loop itself.

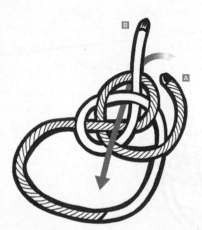

STEP 5

Take End B and bring it down to the left, then pass it back under the last-formed loop, on the lower left-hand side, and under the two lines which cross in the center of this loop. In similar manner to step 4, bring it up through the center of the knot and over the crossed lines and loop on the other side.

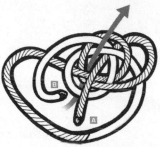

Taking care to ensure that the four loops of the knot remain equal in size, and that the knot retains its shape, pull the two working ends to tighten the knot. Leave flat to use for decorative purposes, or pull the working ends completely tight to use as a stopper knot.

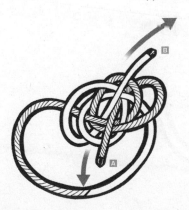

CHAPTER EIGHT
TRICK AND FANCY KNOTS

TRICK & FANCY KNOTS

CHAPTER EIGHT

TRICK AND FANCY KNOTS

Knots can fall into the trick knot category for a variety of reasons. Some do so because they are tied in a particularly impressive manner or unusually quickly; others will unravel when pulled in one direction, but not another. Yet more unravel in a spectacular fashion when placed under strain, while some are "problem-solving" knots—namely, knots that can be tied to provide a solution to a riddle or to meet a particular or unusual need. Some fit several of the above criteria. Fancy knots, meanwhile, are those either tied in an elaborate way or which look particularly impressive or decorative when completed. Several of the knots included here fall into both categories.

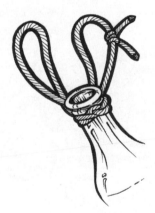

While "problem-solving" trick knots have practical applications, it is also interesting to note that several of the other knots—even those that are designed to unravel easily or which rely on similar shortcomings for their "trick" status—also have their own unique uses in the real world. These uses cover the entire knotting spectrum, as the knots included in this section come from several of the categories already covered, such as hitches, bends, binding knots, and loops.

The trick knots' various origins are as diverse as the knots themselves. Some were discovered by accident while new variations on basic knot structures were being devised. Others were being used for practical purposes when their suitability for entertainment purposes was noted as a secondary characteristic. As with a great number of the knots covered in this book, many trick knots were developed by sailors of centuries past, who used them to while away spare time at sea, and it was aboard ships that many such knots found their uses—some practical, some decorative. Indeed, trick knots have even been uncovered in some of the world's most prestigious archives: Clifford Ashley, for example, discovered some that had been recorded in ethnographic reports by the Smithsonian Institute in Washington, DC.

It should come as no surprise to find that some of the knots in this section are harder to tie than others—many of the easier ones may also require considerable practice to master in their "trick" form. Almost all can be tied with almost any type of material, although anything too thick or too thin may make trick demonstrations more difficult. The only exceptions are those tricks in which a heavy load is placed on the line once the knot has been tied. In these cases, only line that has been verified as strong enough for the purpose at hand should be used, and great care should always be taken to ensure the safety of whoever is demonstrating the trick, as well as any spectators.

GRIEF KNOT

DIFFICULTY: ★ ★ ★ ★

HISTORY

Related to the Reef Knot, the Granny Knot, and the Thief Knot, the Grief Knot dates back a number of centuries, as does its use in rope trickery. Indeed, the four knots are sometimes referred to collectively as "Reef, Grief, Granny, and Thief," and all share the same characteristics in terms of basic structure.

TRICK/FANCY USES

The Grief Knot has many of the failings common to the Granny Knot, although in this case it is these same failings—namely, the ability to come undone under tension thanks to its being "diagonally unbalanced"—that make it a successful trick knot. Unlike the Granny Knot, however, the Grief Knot unravels in a rather spectacular manner, with each line feeding back through the coils of the knot before coming loose. That said, the knot does also have a few practical uses that don't focus on it coming undone, such as holding very light or temporary structures in place (it is technically a binding knot). It can be told apart from the Granny Knot at a glance by the fact that its two ends protrude from the knot on opposite sides; in the Granny Knot, they emerge on the same side.

HOW TO MAKE A
GRIEF KNOT

The Grief Knot is tied as follows:

STEP 1

Taking the working end of the line on your right (Line A), bend it down and under its own working part to create a bight. Take the working end of the line to your left (Line B), and pass it through the bight, going first under, then over.

STEP 2

Take the working end of Line B first under, then back over the working end of Line A, before bringing it up under and over the standing part of Line A. Pass the working end of Line B first under, then over the standing part of Line A.

STEP 3

Carefully pull both working ends to fashion the knot into its correct form.

THIEF KNOT

DIFFICULTY: ★ ☆ ☆ ☆

HISTORY

As Grief Knot is to Granny Knot, so Thief Knot is to Reef Knot. Legend has it that the Thief Knot was invented centuries ago by sailors who kept their possessions tied in cloth bags; if the bag was tied with a Thief Knot, and somebody went rustling through its contents, the chances were that they would not notice the subtle differences of the Thief Knot and would actually retie a Reef Knot by mistake. The bag's owner would later know that his possessions had been rifled through. The knot is also occasionally known as a Bag Knot or a Bread Bag Knot, a result of the above story sometimes being told with the bags in question containing provisions such as bread, rather than personal possessions.

TRICK/FANCY USES

The Thief Knot qualifies as a trick knot in that it can be used to trick someone into thinking it is a Reef Knot, although under careful inspection the two can be told apart in the same way as the Grief and Granny Knot: in a Reef Knot, the ends emerge on opposite sides of the knot, while in a Thief Knot they emerge on the same side. It is structurally a binding knot, but it is known to spill or jam, and as such is fairly useless for anything more strenuous than holding closed a cloth bag.

HOW TO MAKE A THIEF KNOT

As expected, the Thief Knot's creation is similar to that of other members in its family. It is tied as follows:

STEP 1

Bring the working end of the line on your right (Line A) down under its standing part to create a bight. Take the working end of the line on your left (Line B) and pass it through the bight, going first under, then over.

STEP 2

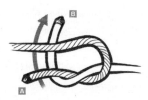

Bring the working end of Line B under both the working end and standing part of Line A.

STEP 3

Moving it toward your left, pass the working end of Line B first over, then under the standing part of Line A. Pull both working ends to tighten.

TRICK & FANCY KNOTS

TOM FOOL'S KNOT

DIFFICULTY: ★ ☆ ☆ ☆

HISTORY

The Tom Fool's Knot is presumably so named because anyone allowing themselves to be tied with it was technically a "Tom Fool," as it was reputedly inescapable, even when used on the most accomplished of escape artists. It is sometimes referred to as the Conjuror's Knot due to its use by those same escape artists on stage, and is related to the Handcuff Knot, the form of which it strongly resembles.

TRICK/FANCY USES

In spite of the legend, the Tom Fool's Knot is far from inescapable—the Handcuff Knot is a far better knot with which to restrain someone—but its trick knot status is assured thanks to the speed and ease with which it can be tied. The Tom Fool's Knot is a loop knot, and can be used as the basis of the Sheepshank; indeed, one of its original uses may well have been to tether more docile farm animals, which would have found it significantly harder to escape than most humans would have done.

HOW TO MAKE A
TOM FOOL'S KNOT

The Tom Fool's Knot is a loop knot tied in the bight as follows:

STEP 1

Lay your line flat in front of you. Take the working end on your left and use it to form a clockwise underhand loop (Loop A). Take the working end on your right and make a counterclockwise overhand loop (Loop B).

STEP 2

Move the loops together so that they overlap, with Loop B on top of Loop A.

STEP 3

Taking hold of each loop where it overlaps the other, pull the edge of each through the other. Pull on the loops to tighten.

TURK'S HEAD

DIFFICULTY: ★★☆☆

HISTORY

The Turk's Head derives its name from its shape, which is said to resemble a turban of the type commonly worn throughout the Eastern world at the time when the knot was created. The knot's invention is widely credited to sailors of the eighteenth century, although the knot did in fact appear much earlier—in the drawings of none other than Leonardo da Vinci in the fifteenth century. Some knot scholars have also noted that America's cowboys used knots very similar to the Turk's Head, and that these originated in Spanish South America.

TRICK/FANCY USES

Aboard ships, the Turk's Head had one important purpose: it was tied onto the upper middle of the wheel to make it obvious when the boat was being steered in a straight line. This practice, known as "marking the king spoke," was extremely useful for a number of reasons; most notably, it allowed the person steering to judge direction even at night or in periods of poor visibility. The great bulk of the knot also meant that it could be easily found by hand, aiding steering even in severe storms or periods of virtual blindness.

The knot was also used for various other purposes, including as a grip on ladders and guard rails, for the sealing of bags and even to secure anklets and bracelets. As such, the knot qualifies as both a trick knot and a fancy knot, the latter status guaranteed by its highly decorative appearance, and these days it can still be found in many intricate jewelry designs. From a trick point of view, the knot enthusiast can impress their audience with their vast knowledge of the numerous variations on the Turk's Head—which in fact constitutes an entire family of knots, rather than just one.

Even more impressive would be an understanding of the mathematical formulae employed to plan a Turk's Head in advance. Any Turk's Head knot is said to have a number of "leads"—namely, the number of times the line crosses as it goes around whatever object it has been tied around. The knot will also have a number of "bends" or "bights"—in this case, the number of times the line crosses itself along that same object's long axis (Turk's Head knots always being tied around a cylindrical object). The formulae come into play when the knot is to be tied with multiple strands of line: the number of strands will always be the same as the largest common factor of the number of leads and the number of bends, and any audience is sure to be impressed by the demonstrator having worked these numbers out in advance.

It should also be noted that there are three varieties of Turk's Head—another fact that can be used to wow an audience. The knots are said to be "narrow" when there are two or more fewer leads than there are bends, "square" in cases where the number of leads or bends is one greater than the other, or "wide" when there are two or more fewer bends than leads. It is not possible to tie a Turk's Head with an equal number of bends and leads.

HOW TO MAKE A
TURK'S HEAD

As already mentioned, there are a great many variations on the Turk's Head Knot. The knot is usually tied around something (like a wheel rim or gang rail), but it can also be tied flat and then placed around a cylindrical object, and it is this most basic version that is described here:

STEP 1

Placing the line flat in front of you, bring both working ends down to create a bight. Take the working end on your right (End A) over the standing part of the working end on your left (End B), then bring it up and back over End B's standing part and its own. You should now have two overlapping loops.

STEP 2

Take End B in hand, and bring it over End A. Take it through the loop on your right, going under the right edge and over the standing part of End A where it bisects the loop, under the left edge and then over the most extreme left edge of the loop to your left.

STEP 3

The resulting structure will consist of one large loop at the top center and two smaller ones on the left and right, through which the working ends pass. Take End B, which will now be on your left, and pass it through the lowest central part of the loop to your right, going first under, then over the line bisecting this loop. This completes the form of the Turk's Head, and should give you four outer "loops." By placing your fingers in the center of the knot and adjusting the line outward, the size of these loops can be adjusted and the ends made fast. This can also be placed around a post and pulled tight by pulling the ends.

SHEEPSHANK KNOT

DIFFICULTY: ★★☆☆

HISTORY

The Sheepshank is a shortening knot—it allows slack to be taken up out of a line and removes unwanted length, giving it the added benefit of being adjustable and so used to vary the length of the line in which it is tied. Legend has it that the knot is named after its original use for tying sheep to individual wooden posts while they grazed. The rope would give each sheep only a certain circular amount of grass on which to feed; when the sheep had consumed all the grass within that area, its tether could be made longer by quick manipulation of the Sheepshank, thus giving it more room to graze.

TRICK/FANCY USES

For practical purposes, the Sheepshank is useful for shortening a line—for example, if the user wishes to remove undue strain from any part of a rope or cord that he or she thinks may have been damaged by past wear. There are several ways of tying a Sheepshank, and the method described here is the "trick" version, qualifying as such thanks to the way in which tying it consists of fluid, seemingly simultaneous movements of previously prepared loops in the line.

HOW TO MAKE A SHEEPSHANK

The "trick" Sheepshank is tied as follows:

STEP 1

Bring the working end on your right up and under the standing part to create a clockwise underhand loop in the center of your line. Next, bring the end up and under the standing part again to create a second, smaller clockwise underhand loop to the right of the first.

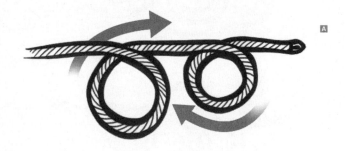

TRICK & FANCY KNOTS

STEP 2

Take the working end to your left and bring this up and over the standing part to create a similar counterclockwise overhand loop to the left of the central loop, positioning it so that it is underneath and overlapped by the left edge of the central loop. Similarly, position the right-hand loop so that it is on top of and overlapping the center loop.

STEP 3

Anchoring down the working ends, take hold of the left and right edges of the central loop. Simultaneously pull the left edge through the left side loop, taking it under the leftmost edge, and pull the right edge through the right side loop, taking it over the rightmost edge. This should execute a perfect Sheepshank.

TRICK & FANCY KNOTS

SLIPPERY HITCH

DIFFICULTY: ★★★★

HISTORY

As Clifford Ashley noted in his famous *Ashley Book of Knots*, the Slippery Hitch (or Slipped Half Hitch) is the answer to a riddle. The riddle poses a simple question: how can someone use a length of rope to get down from a cliff that has a tree or other solid anchor point at its edge, yet still walk away with the rope once they have landed on solid ground?

TRICK/FANCY USES

The trickery inherent in the Slippery Hitch stems from the fact that it is stable when weight is applied to one end, but comes undone when the other is pulled. In relation to the above riddle, therefore, this means that it can be used to get down from the cliff in question and then pulled undone from the bottom, thus impressing onlookers (although a cliff with an anchoring tree is not necessary for the demonstration— a smaller and preferably safer setup will suffice). Practically speaking, the Slippery Hitch has a few other uses: it can be employed to tether small, light boats (which leads to it being occasionally known as the Canoe Hitch), while the fact that it can be so easily released leads some to use it for securing sails to small sailboats.

HOW TO MAKE A
SLIPPERY HITCH

Technically, the Slippery Hitch is a slipped version of the Clove Hitch. It is tied as follows:

STEP 1

Loop your line around the object to which you wish to anchor it. Take the working end on your left (End A) and pass it under the standing part of the working end on your right (End B).

STEP 2

Next, bring End A up and back over End B's standing part, then under its own. You should now have a completed Half Hitch. Do not pull tight at this stage.

STEP 3

Bring End A up to form a bight before passing it back through the center of the knot—where it goes around your anchor object—taking it under the left line of this and over the right. Making sure to leave the loop that this creates to your left, take hold of End A and pull End B to tighten.

STEP 4

Weight can now be placed on End B without the knot coming undone, but pulling on End A will immediately release the knot. In Ashley's theoretical cliff situation, plenty of length would be left in the standing parts of both ends to reach the bottom of the precipice. You could then climb down the cliff using the standing part of End B before pulling on the standing part of End A to release the knot, and then pulling the newly loosened rope down after you.

MONKEY'S FIST

DIFFICULTY: ★ ★ ★ ★

HISTORY

Fascinating both to look at and to make, the Monkey's Fist was invented for purely practical purposes by sailors some time before the nineteenth century.

At the time of its invention, when all boats were sail-based and powered by wind alone, it was hard to move ships together in emergency circumstances—to offer assistance when another craft was coming under attack by pirates, for example. The obvious answer to this problem was for the crew of one ship to throw rope lines to the other, and for everyone to then pull on these and thus draw the two boats together; the only problem was that the ropes were so light, they seldom reached the other ship when thrown.

The solution came with the practice of weighing down the ends of these lines (referred to as "heaving lines"), making them heavy enough to counteract the effects of wind resistance, and sail through the air and reach the other boat safely. Then the sailors needed a knot capable of securely holding a heavy object such as a stone to the end of the line, and the Monkey's Fist was perfect.

The knot's enigmatic name is derived from its shape, which does indeed resemble a fist of sorts, and is also a nod to the fact that a monkey, when clutching something in its hand, tends not to release it voluntarily. For this reason, it was often joked that the best way to catch a monkey was to place an object inside a jar. The monkey would then reach into the jar to clasp the object; unable to remove its hand from the jar without in turn releasing the object, the monkey would thus find itself trapped.

Whether or not this method of monkey catching works is very much open to debate, but there's little doubt that the Monkey's Fist knot certainly worked for the sailors of the time, who also used it to weigh down lines that were then thrown to rescue people foundering in the open ocean. The knot was first documented by name in E. N. Little's *Log Book Notes of 1888*, although Little didn't give any actual instructions for tying the knot itself. Indeed, the earliest documented directions for constructing a Monkey's Fist knot didn't appear until almost a century later, when Cyrus Laurence Day wrote them down in his 1935 book, *Sailor's Knots*.

TRICK/FANCY USES

The Monkey's Fist's original use has been well documented, but, although weighing down a line may once have been a matter of life and death, these days it is more likely to be part of a performance trick. That said, the act of making a Monkey's Fist alone is something of an impressive feat; while not difficult in itself, the end result does look rather spectacular.

A line with a Monkey's Fist tied into it is also surprisingly useful in all sorts of unusual situations. Extreme climbers have been known to use them to help get single ropes over unusual rock formations before ascending them. In a more purely aesthetic application, the Maori people of New Zealand use the knot in the practice Poi, a type of juggling with balls attached to the ends of short ropes. Originally used to develop strength and dexterity, Poi is now a ritualistic tradition amongst modern Maori tribes.

In addition to these uses, the Monkey's Fist can also be used purely for decoration. It is often found suspended from necklaces, key rings, earrings, cufflinks, and the like, thus also qualifying it as a fancy knot. In the United States, it has been adopted by the homeless community as a symbol of brotherhood and solidarity, and some homeless charities raise money by selling pieces of jewelry depicting the Monkey's Fist, many of them handcrafted by homeless people themselves.

HOW TO MAKE A MONKEY'S FIST

While it is generally tied around a central core to help develop its shape, the Monkey's Fist can also be tied on its own. When not using a core, additional turns should be made to ensure the knot retains its form, a practice that should also be employed when using a lighter or less solid core.

STEP 1

Take the working end of your line and make three turns in it, going over, under, over, under, over, and then under again.

STEP 2

Pass the working end around the center of these turns in a similar fashion three times, so that these subsequent turns are at right angles to the first three. On the final exit, pass the working end through the center of the turns.

STEP 3

Place your core (if one is being used) into the center of what you have just created. Pass the working end back under the core and up and over the second series of turns another three times, going around the core and under the original turns each time. Trim any excess from the working end if necessary.

TRICK & FANCY KNOTS

BOTTLE SLING

DIFFICULTY: ★★★★

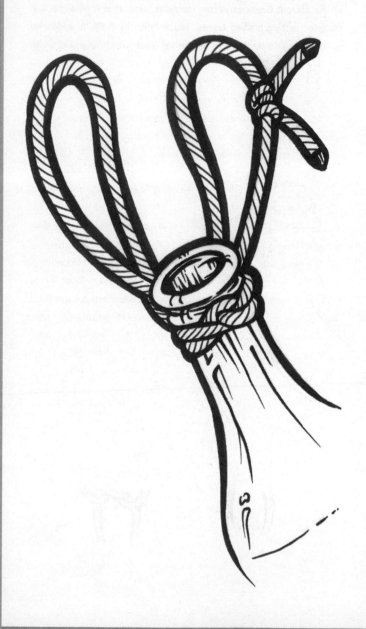

HISTORY

Variously referred to as the Bottle Sling, Jug Sling, Jar Sling, or Hackamore Knot (when tied in doubled line), this particular knot is one of the earliest ever recorded, first mentioned in the writings of the ancient Greek physician Heraklas, who used it as a medical sling for setting broken bones. Much later, in 1888, it appeared in the book *Log Book Notes* as the Jar Sling, which was said to be most popularly used for holding jugs, pitchers, and other vessels—a purpose that many claim the ancient Greeks also employed it for. Either way, the Bottle Sling also makes a memorable appearance in the *Ashley Book of Knots*, in which author Clifford Ashley relates a story about how he demonstrated the knot's strength by swinging the slung bottle over his head, terrifying the owner of the Cape Cod store he happened to be in at the time.

TRICK/FANCY USES

The Bottle Sling is a trick knot for several reasons. First, as Ashley proved, when tied properly it is so secure that it can be used to safely whirl a bottle around at height. Second, the mere act of tying it demands a certain level of dexterity—particularly in finishing the knot off properly. Finally, its ability to hold fast bottles, pitchers, and jars can be especially pleasing to a captive audience—not least when those bottles are filled with beverages and then slung over the side of a small boat for cooling in the water below.

HOW TO MAKE
A BOTTLE SLING

Any whirling around of bottles should be done only where safe to do so, and with cord that is indisputably strong enough to withstand the strain. The Bottle Sling is tied as follows:

STEP 1

Placing your line flat in front of you, use the working end on your right to make a counterclockwise underhand loop (Loop A). Take the left working end, and use this to make a clockwise underhand loop (Loop B) to the left of Loop A. Position Loop A so that it overlaps Loop B.

STEP 2

Both working ends should now point downward. Keep hold of these, and take hold of the line where it crosses the standing parts of both working ends. Pull this bight under the standing part to your left, taking it first through Loop B, and then through the area where the two loops overlap, going first over, then under; it should thus exit through Loop A. Bring it over the far right edge of Loop A so that it now stands at the top center of the structure so far.

STEP 3

The top edge of Loop A should now be the highest line crossing this top bight, passing behind it. Taking hold of this, pull it down behind the knot to where the standing parts emerge

STEP 4

The top edge of Loop B should now be the highest line crossing this top bight, passing in front of it. Taking hold of this, pull it down in front of the knot to where the standing parts emerge.

STEP 5

The bottle neck can now be placed into the center of the knot, and the loop at the top and the working ends pulled to tighten the knot around it. To make secure, one of the working ends should then be passed through the loop and tied to the other using a secure bend.